Other Regal Books on This Theme:

Edited by Fritz Ridenour
"How to Be a Christian Without Being Religious"
Comments on the important questions of life which face every individual. Uses as a basis the New Testament book of Romans in the fresh contemporary language of the *Living Letters* paraphrase. Liberally illustrated with incisive cartoons.

By H. S. Vigeveno.
"Jesus the Revolutionary"
Penetrating, forceful, this book unmasks the living, compelling Jesus of the Bible.

By J. Edwin Orr
"100 Questions About God"
A candid, dynamic dialogue about the nature and works of God.

By Henrietta C. Mears
"What the Bible Is All About"
An easy-to-understand survey of the Bible.

THE MAN JESUS

THE MAN JESUS

Co-published by

Regal Books, G/L Publications
Glendale, California, U.S.A.

Tyndale House, Publishers
Wheaton, Illinois, U.S.A.

Over 200,000 in print

Library of Congress Catalog Card No. 67-27444
Paperback Edition: ISBN-0-8307-0068-4
Casebound Edition: ISBN-0-8307-0074-9

Second Printing, 1968
Third Printing, 1969
Fourth Printing, 1969
Fifth Printing, 1970
Sixth Printing, 1970
Seventh Printing, 1971
Eighth Printing, 1972

Co-published by

Regal Books, G/L Publications
Glendale, California, U.S.A.

Tyndale House, Publishers
Wheaton, Illinois, U.S.A.

Contents

Preface

The life of Jesus has attracted more attention, more questions and answers than that of anyone else who ever walked the earth.

Now you can read the story of Jesus' life as you have never read it before. Here is the complete story of his life on earth in one continuous narrative: a single account of all the events recorded by the four Gospel writers—without omission, without duplication. The text is a paraphrase not an exact translation. It is taken from *Living Gospels* by Kenneth N. Taylor, published by Tyndale House, 1966.

The only changes in the text are those required to show the passage of time or the change of location. In the account of the death and resurrection of Jesus, the pronouns have been changed from the first to the third person to provide a uniformity of style.

Dates have been included to help you to get a feeling of continuity and of the lapse of time. These are of course approximate but as close as possible to the correct time. The dates are taken from the *Holy Bible, The Berkeley Version*, published by Zondervan Publishing House, 1946, and used by permission.

As you read the order in which the events took place you will find their authenticity emphasized. Familiar stories will fit into place as a perspective of time develops. Episodes will assume a new relevance as you read them in their proper sequence. The importance of certain phases of Jesus' life will be more fully realized as you see the amount of detail given to their description. Here, then, is the true story of the life of the one who drastically and irrevocably changed the course of history.

Whose son is he?

PART 1

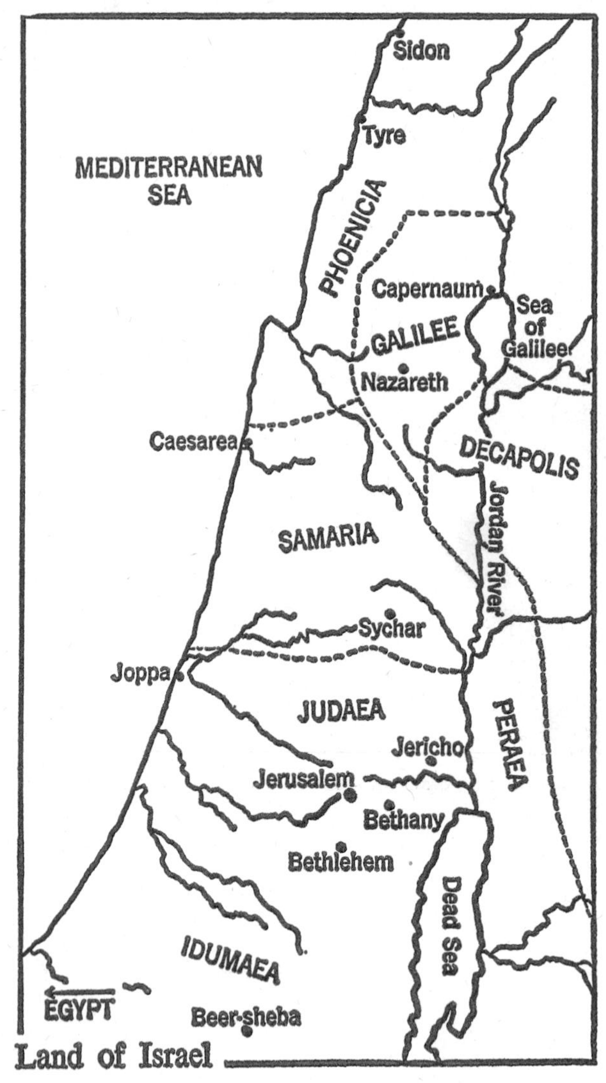

Land of Israel

Chapter 1

Before the Beginning

Before anything else existed, there was Christ,* with God. He has always been alive and is Himself God. He created everything there is—nothing exists that He didn't make. Eternal life is in Him, and this life gives light to all mankind. His life is the light that shines through the darkness—and the darkness can never extinguish it.

Several accounts of Christ's life have already been written using as their source material the reports circulating among us from the early disciples and other eyewitnesses. However, it occurred to me that it would be well to recheck all these accounts from first to last and after thorough investigation to pass this summary on to you so that you may be reassured of the truth of all you were taught.

Around September, 6 B.C.

My story begins with a Jewish priest, Zacharias, who lived when Herod was king of Judea. Zacharias was a member of the Abijah division of the Temple service corps. His wife Elizabeth was also a member of the priest tribe of the Jews, being a descendant of Aaron. Zacharias and

John 1:1-5; Luke 1:1-6

*Literally, "the Word," meaning Christ, the wisdom and power of God and the first cause of all things; God's personal expression of Himself to men.

Elizabeth were godly folk, careful to obey all of God's laws—in spirit as well as in letter. But they had no children, for Elizabeth was barren; and now they were very old.

One day as Zacharias was going about his work in the Temple—for his division was on duty that week—the honor fell to him by lot to enter the inner sanctuary and burn incense before the Lord. Meanwhile, a great crowd stood outside in the Temple court, praying as they always did during that part of the service when the incense was being burned. Zacharias was in the sanctuary when suddenly an angel appeared, standing to the right of the altar of incense! Zacharias was startled and terrified.

But the angel said, "Don't be afraid, Zacharias! For I have come to tell you that God has heard your prayer, and your wife, Elizabeth, will bear you a son! And you are to name him John! You will have great joy and gladness at his birth, and many will rejoice with you. For he will be one of the Lord's great men. He must never touch wine or strong drink—and he will be filled with the Holy Spirit, even from before his birth! And he will persuade many a Jew to turn to the Lord his God. He will be a man of rugged spirit and power, like Elijah, the prophet of old; and he will precede the coming of the Messiah, preparing the people for His arrival. He will teach them to love the Lord, just as their ancestors did, and to live as godly men."

Luke 1:6-17

Zacharias said to the angel, "But how can I be sure of this? For I am an old man now, and my wife is also well along in years."

Then the angel said, "I am Gabriel! I stand in the very presence of God. It was He who sent me to bring you this good news! And now because you haven't believed me, you are to be stricken silent, unable to speak until the child is born. For my words will certainly come true at the proper time!"

Meanwhile, the crowds outside were waiting for Zacharias to come out, and wondered why he was taking so long. When he finally appeared, he couldn't speak to them; and they realized from his gestures that he must have seen a vision in the Temple. He then fulfilled the remaining days of his Temple duties and returned home.

Soon afterwards Elizabeth his wife became pregnant, and went into seclusion for five months. "How kind the Lord is," she exclaimed, "to take away my disgrace of having no children!"

Around March, 5 B.C.

The following month God sent the angel Gabriel to Nazareth, a village in Galilee, to a virgin, Mary, engaged to be married to a man named Joseph, a descendant of King David. Gabriel appeared to her and said, "Congratulations, favored lady! The Lord is with you!" Confused and disturbed, she

Luke 1:18-29

tried to think what he could mean.

"Don't be frightened, Mary," the angel said, "for God has decided to wonderfully bless you! Very soon now, you will become pregnant and have a baby boy, and you are to name Him 'Jesus.' He shall be very great and shall be called the Son of God. And the Lord God shall give Him the throne of His ancestor David. And He shall reign over Israel forever; His Kingdom shall never end!"

Mary asked the angel, "But how can I have a baby? I am a virgin."

The angel replied, "The Holy Spirit shall come upon you, and the power of God shall overshadow you; so the baby born to you will be utterly holy—the Son of God. Furthermore, six months ago your cousin Elizabeth—'the barren one,' they called her—became pregnant in her old age! For every promise from God shall surely come true."

Mary said, "I am the Lord's servant, and I am willing to do whatever He says. May everything come true as you have told me." And then the angel disappeared.

A few days later Mary hurried to the highlands of Judea to the town where Zacharias lived, to visit Elizabeth. At the sound of Mary's greeting, Elizabeth's child leaped within her and she was filled with the Holy Spirit!

She gave a glad cry and exclaimed to Mary, "You are favored by God above all other women, and your child is destined for God's mightiest

Luke 1:29-42

praise. What an honor this is, that the mother of my Lord should visit me! When you came in and greeted me, the instant I heard your voice, my baby moved in me for joy! You believed that God would do what He said; that is why He has given you this wonderful blessing."

Mary responded, "Oh, how I praise the Lord! How I rejoice in God my Savior! For He took notice of His lowly servant girl, and now generation after generation forever shall call me blest of God! For He, the mighty Holy One, has done great things to me. His mercy goes on from generation to generation to all who reverence Him. How powerful is His mighty arm! How He scatters the proud and haughty ones! He has torn princes from their thrones and exalted the lowly. He has satisfied the hungry hearts and sent the rich away with empty hands. And how He has helped His servant Israel! He has not forgotten His promise to be merciful. For He promised our fathers—Abraham and his children—to be merciful to them forever."

Mary stayed with Elizabeth about three months and then went back to her own home.

When Mary became pregnant by the Holy Spirit, Joseph, her fiancé, being a man of stern principle, decided to break the engagement but to do it quietly, as he didn't want to publicly disgrace her.

As he lay awake considering this, he fell into a dream, and saw an angel standing beside him.

Luke 1:42-56; Matthew 1:18-20

"Joseph, son of David," the angel said, "don't hesitate to take Mary as your wife! For the child within her has been conceived by the Holy Spirit! And she will have a son, and you shall name Him Jesus (meaning 'Savior'), for He will save His people from their sins. This will fulfill God's message through His prophets—'Listen! The virgin shall conceive a child! She shall give birth to a son, and he shall be called "Emmanuel" (meaning "God is with us").' "

When Joseph awoke, he did as the angel commanded, and brought Mary home to be his wife, but she remained a virgin until her son was born.

Around June, 5 B.C.

By now Elizabeth's waiting was over, for the time had come for the baby to be born—and it was a boy! The word spread quickly to her neighbors and relatives of how kind the Lord had been to her, and everyone rejoiced.

When the baby was eight days old, all the relatives and friends came for the circumcision ceremony. They all assumed the baby's name would be Zacharias, after his father. But Elizabeth said, "No! He must be named John!"

"What?" they exclaimed. "There is no one in all your family by that name!"

So they asked the baby's father, talking to him by gestures. He motioned for a piece of paper and

Matthew 1:20-25; Luke 1:57-62

to everyone's surprise wrote, "His name is John!" Instantly Zacharias could speak again, and he began praising God!

Wonder fell upon the whole neighborhood, and the news of what had happened spread through the Judean hills. And everyone who heard about it thought long thoughts and asked, "I wonder what this child will turn out to be?" The hand of the Lord was surely upon him in some special way.

Then his father Zacharias was filled with the Holy Spirit and gave this prophecy: "Praise the Lord, the God of Israel, for He has come to visit His people and has redeemed them. He is sending us a Mighty Savior from the royal line of His servant David just as He promised through His holy prophets long ago—someone to save us from our enemies, from all who hate us; He has been merciful to our ancestors, yes, to Abraham himself, by remembering His sacred promise to him and by granting us the privilege of serving God fearlessly, freed from our enemies, and by making us holy and acceptable, ready to stand in His presence forever.

"And you, my little son, shall be called the prophet of the glorious God, for you will prepare the way for the Messiah. You will tell His people how to find salvation by forgiveness of their sins. All this will be because the mercy of our God is very tender, and heaven's dawn is about to break

Luke 1:62-78

upon us, to give light to those who sit in darkness and death's shadow, and to guide us to the path of peace."

Luke 1:78, 79

Flight to Egypt

Chapter 2

Few Know, Fewer Care

Around December, 5 B.C.

About that time Caesar Augustus, the Roman Emperor, decreed that a census should be taken throughout the empire. This census was taken when Quirinius was governor of Syria. Everyone was required to return to his ancestral home for the registration. And because Joseph was a member of the royal line, he had to go to Bethlehem in Judea, King David's ancient home—journeying there from the Galilean city of Nazareth. He took with him Mary who was obviously pregnant by that time.

And while they were there, the time came for her baby to be born; and she gave birth to her first child, a son. She wrapped Him in a blanket and laid Him in a manger, because there was no room for them in the village inn.

That night some shepherds were in the fields outside the village, guarding their flocks of sheep. Suddenly an angel appeared among them, and the landscape shone bright with the glory of the Lord. They were badly frightened, but the angel reassured them. "Don't be afraid!" he said. "I bring you the most joyful news ever announced, and it is for everyone! The Savior—yes, the Messiah, the Lord

Luke: 2:1-11

—has been born today in Bethlehem! How will you recognize Him? You will find a baby wrapped in a blanket, lying in a manger!"

Suddenly, the angel was joined by a vast host of others—the armies of heaven—praising God: "Glory to God in the highest heaven," they sang, "and peace on earth for all those pleasing Him."

When this great army of angels had returned again to heaven, the shepherds said to each other, "Come on! Let's go to Bethlehem! Let's see this wonderful thing that has happened, which the Lord has told us about." They ran to the village and found their way to Mary and Joseph. And there was the baby, lying in the manger!

The shepherds told everyone what had happened and what the angel had said to them about this child. Everyone who heard the shepherds' story expressed astonishment, but Mary quietly treasured all these things in her heart and often thought about them. Then the shepherds went back to their fields and flocks again, praising God for the visit of the angels and because they had seen the child, just as the angel had told them they would.

Eight days later at the baby's circumcision ceremony, He was named Jesus, the name given Him by the angel before He was even conceived.

January—February, 4 B.C.

When the time came for Mary's purification offer-

Luke 2:11-22

ing at the Temple, as required by the laws of Moses after the birth of a child, His parents took Him to Jerusalem to present Him to the Lord, for in these laws God had said, "If a woman's first child is a boy, he shall be dedicated to the Lord." At that time Jesus' parents also offered their sacrifice for purification—"either a pair of turtledoves or two young pigeons" was the legal requirement.

That day a man named Simeon, who lived in Jerusalem, was in the Temple. He was a good man, very devout, filled with the Holy Spirit and constantly expecting the Messiah to come soon. For the Holy Spirit had revealed to him that he would not die until he had seen Him—God's anointed King. The Holy Spirit had impelled him to go to the Temple that day; and so, when Mary and Joseph arrived to present the baby Jesus to the Lord in obedience to the law, Simeon was there and took Him in his arms, praising God.

"Lord," he said, "now I can die content! For I have seen Him as You promised me I would! I have seen the Savior You have given to the world! He is the Light that will shine upon the nations, and He will be the glory of Your people Israel!"

Joseph and Mary just stood there, marveling at what was being said about Jesus. Simeon blessed them but then said to Mary, His mother, "A sword shall pierce your soul, for this child shall be rejected by many in Israel, and this to their undoing. But He will be the greatest joy of many others. And

Luke 2:22-35

the deepest thoughts of many hearts shall be revealed."

Anna, a prophetess, was also there in the Temple that day. She was the daughter of Phanuel, of the Jewish tribe of Asher, and was very old, for she had been a widow for 84 years following seven years of marriage. She never left the Temple but stayed there night and day, worshiping God by praying, and often going without food. She came along just as Simeon was talking with Mary and Joseph, and she also began thanking God and publicly proclaiming the Messiah's arrival to everyone in Jerusalem who had been awaiting the coming of the Savior.

Luke 2:35-38

Chapter 3

Half a World Away

Jesus was born in the town of Bethlehem, in Judea, during the reign of King Herod. At about that time some astrologers from eastern lands arrived in Jerusalem, asking, "Where is the newborn King of the Jews? for we have seen His star in far-off eastern lands, and have come to worship Him."

King Herod was deeply disturbed by their question, and all Jerusalem was filled with rumors. He called a meeting of all the Jewish religious leaders. "Did the prophets tell us where the Messiah would be born?" he asked.

"Yes, in Bethlehem," they said, "for this is what the prophet Micah wrote: 'O little town of Bethlehem, you are not just an unimportant Judean village, for a Governor shall rise from you to rule My people Israel.'"

Then Herod sent a secret message to the astrologers, asking them to come see him; and he found out from them the exact time of the star's first appearance. "Go to Bethlehem," he told them, "and search for the child. And when you find Him, come back and tell me, so that I can worship Him too!"

The astrologers listened and then left. And look! The star appeared again, standing over Bethlehem.

Matthew 2:1-9

Their joy knew no bounds! Entering the house where the baby and Mary His mother were, they fell to the floor before Him, worshiping. Then they opened their presents and gave Him gold, frankincense and myrrh.

And when they returned to their own land, they didn't go through Jerusalem to report to Herod, for God had warned them in a dream to go home another way.

After they were gone, Joseph dreamed again, and again an angel of the Lord appeared to him. "Get up and flee to Egypt with the baby and His mother," the angel said, "and stay there until I tell you to return, for King Herod is going to try to kill the child." That same night he left for Egypt with Mary and the baby and stayed there until King Herod's death. This fulfilled the prophet's prediction, "I have called My Son from Egypt."

Herod was furious when he realized that the astrologers had deceived him. Sending soldiers to Bethlehem, he ordered them to kill every baby boy two years old and under, both in the town and on the nearby farms, for the astrologers had told him the star first appeared to them two years before.

This brutal action of Herod's fulfilled the prophecy of Jeremiah, "Screams of anguish come from Ramah, weeping unrestrained; Rachel weeping for her children, uncomforted—for they are dead."

Matthew 2:10-18

Chapter 4

The Silent Time

When Herod died, an angel of the Lord appeared in a dream to Joseph in Egypt, and told him, "Arise and take the baby and His mother back to Israel, for those who sought to kill the child are dead."

So he returned immediately to Israel with Jesus and His mother. But on the way he was frightened to learn that the new king was Herod's son Archelaus. Then, in another dream, he was warned not to go to Jerusalem, so they went to Galilee instead and lived in Nazareth. This fulfilled the prediction of the prophets concerning the Messiah, "He shall be called a Nazarene."

There the child became a strong, robust lad, and was known for wisdom beyond His years; and God poured out His blessings on Him.

April, A.D. 8 or 9

When Jesus was 12 years old, He accompanied His parents to Jerusalem for the annual Passover Festival, which they attended each year. After the celebration was over, they started home to Nazareth, but Jesus stayed behind in Jerusalem. They didn't miss Him the first day, for they assumed He

Matthew 2:19-23; Luke 2:40-44

was with friends among the other travelers. But when He didn't show up that evening, they started to look for Him among their relatives and friends. When they couldn't find Him, they went back to Jerusalem to search for Him.

Three days later they finally discovered Him in the Temple, sitting among the teachers of Law, discussing deep questions with them and amazing everyone with His understanding and answers. His parents didn't know what to think when they saw Him sitting there with those great men. "Son!" His mother said to Him, "Why have You done this to us? Your father and I have been frantic, searching for You everywhere."

"But why did you need to search?" He asked. "Didn't you realize that I would be here in My Father's House?" But they didn't understand what He meant.

Then He returned to Nazareth with them and was obedient to them; and His mother stored away all these things in her heart. So Jesus grew both tall and wise, and was loved by God and man.

Luke 2:44-52

Chapter 5

Crowds in the Desert

Summer of A.D. 26

In the book written by the prophet Isaiah, God announced that He would send His Son to earth, and that a special messenger would come first to prepare the world for His arrival. "This messenger will live out in the barren wilderness," Isaiah said, "and will proclaim that everyone must straighten out his life to be ready for the Lord's arrival."

This messenger was John the Baptist. When he grew up he lived out in the lonely wilderness until he began his public ministry to Israel.

In the fifteenth year of the reign of the Emperor, Tiberius Caesar, a message came from God to John the son of Zacharias, as he was living out in the deserts. Pilate was governor over Judea at that time; Herod, over Galilee; his brother Philip, over Iturea and Trachonitis; Lysanias, over Abilene; and Annas and Caiaphas were the Jewish high priests.

Then John went from place to place on both sides of the Jordan River, preaching that people should be baptized to show that they had turned to God and away from their sins in order to be forgiven. In the words of Isaiah the prophet, John was "a voice shouting from the barren wilderness,

Mark 1:2-4; Luke 1:80; Luke 3:1-4

'Prepare a road for the Lord to travel on! Widen the pathway before Him! Level the mountains! Fill up the valleys! Straighten the curves! Smooth out the ruts! And then all mankind shall see the Savior sent from God.' "

People from Jerusalem and from all over Judea traveled out into the Judean wastelands to see and hear John, and when they confessed their sins, he baptized them in the Jordan River. His clothes were woven from camel's hair and he wore a leather belt; locusts and wild honey were his food.

Here is a sample of John's preaching to the crowds that came for baptism: "You brood of snakes! You are trying to escape hell without truly turning to God! That is why you want to be baptized! First go and show by the way you live that you really have repented. And don't think you are safe because you are descendants of Abraham. That isn't enough! God can produce children of Abraham from these desert stones! The axe of God's judgment is poised over you, ready to sever your roots and cut you down. Yes, every tree that does not produce good fruit will be chopped down and thrown into the fire."

The crowd replied, "Just what do you want us to do?"

"If you have two coats," he replied, "give one to the poor. If you have extra food, give it away to those who are hungry."

Even tax collectors—notorious for their corrup-

Luke 3:4-6; Mark 1:5,6; Luke 3:7-12

tion—came to be baptized and asked, "How shall we prove to you that we have abandoned our sins?"

"By your honesty," he replied. "Make sure you collect no more taxes than the Roman government requires you to."

"And us," asked some soldiers, "what about us?"

John replied, "Don't extort money by threats and violence; don't accuse anyone of what you know he didn't do; and be content with your pay!"

Everyone was expecting the Messiah to come soon, and eager to know whether or not John was He. This was the question of the hour, and it was discussed everywhere.

John answered the question by saying, "I baptize only with water; but someone is coming soon who has far higher authority than mine; in fact, I am not worthy of being His slave. He will baptize you with fire—with the Holy Spirit. He will separate chaff from grain, and burn up the chaff with eternal fire and store away the grain."

God sent John the Baptist as a witness so that everyone would know Jesus Christ is the true Light. John himself was not the Light; he was only a witness to identify it.

The true Light who shines on everyone was coming into the world. But although He made the world, the world didn't recognize Him when He came. Even in His own land and among His own people, the Jews, He was not accepted. Only a few would welcome and receive Him. But to all who

Luke 3:12-17; John 1:6-12

received Him, He gave the right to become children of God. All they needed to do was believe He would save them. All those who believed this were reborn!—not a physical rebirth, resulting from human passion or plan—but from the will of God. And Christ* became a human being and lived here on earth among us and was full of loving forgiveness and truth. And some of us have seen His glory—the glory of the only Son of the heavenly Father!

Late A.D. 26, or early 27

Then one day Jesus went from Galilee to the Jordan River to be baptized by John. John didn't want to do it. "This isn't proper," he said. "I am the one who needs to be baptized by You."

But Jesus said, "Please do it, for I must do all that is right." So then John baptized Him.

The moment Jesus came up out of the water, He saw the heavens open and the Holy Spirit in the form of a dove descending on Him, and a voice from heaven said, "This is My beloved Son, and I am very pleased with Him."

John pointed Him out to the people, telling the crowds, "This is the one I was talking about when I said, 'Someone is coming who is greater by far than I am—for He existed long before I did!'" We have all benefited from the rich blessings He brought to us—blessing upon blessing heaped upon us! For Moses gave us the Law with its rigid demands and

John 1:12-14; Matt. 3:13-15; Mark 1:10; Matt. 3:17; John 1:15-17

*Literally, "the Word," meaning Christ, the wisdom and power of

merciless justice; Jesus Christ brought us loving forgiveness as well. No one has ever actually seen God, but of course His only Son has, for He is the companion of the Father and has told us all about Him.

The Jewish leaders sent priests and assistant priests from Jerusalem to ask John whether he claimed to be the Messiah. He denied it flatly. "I am not the Christ," he said.

"Well then, who are you?" they asked. "Are you Elijah?"

"No," he replied.

"Are you the Prophet?"

"No."

"Then who are you? Tell us, so we can give an answer to those who sent us. What do you have to say for yourself?"

He replied, "I am a voice from the barren wilderness, shouting as Isaiah prophesied, 'Get ready for the coming of the Lord!' "

Then those who were sent by the Pharisees asked him, "If you aren't the Messiah or Elijah or the Prophet, what right do you have to baptize?"

John told them, "I merely baptize with water, but right here in the crowd is someone you have never met who will soon begin His ministry among you, and I am not fit to be His slave." This incident took place at Bethany, a village on the other side of the Jordan River where John was baptizing.

Jesus, full of the Holy Spirit, left the Jordan

John 1:17-28

River and was urged by the Spirit out into the barren wastelands of Judea, where Satan tempted Him for 40 days. He ate nothing all that time, and was very hungry. Satan said, "If you are God's Son, tell this stone to become a loaf of bread."

But Jesus replied, "It is written in the Scriptures, 'Other things in life are more important than bread!' "

Then Satan took Him to a place where he revealed to Jesus all the kingdoms of the world in a moment of time. And the Devil told Him, "I will give You all these splendid kingdoms and their glory—for they are mine to give to anyone I wish—if You will only get down on Your knees before me and worship me."

Jesus replied, "We must worship God, and Him alone. So it is written in the Scriptures." Then Satan took Him to Jerusalem to a high roof of the Temple and said, "If You are the Son of God, jump off! For the Scriptures say that God will send His angels to guard You and to keep You from crashing to the pavement below!"

Jesus replied, "The Scriptures also say, 'Don't experiment with God's patience!' " When the Devil had ended all the temptations, he left Jesus for a while and went away.

Luke 4:1-13

Chapter 6

Getting Started

Late February or early March, A.D. 27

Jesus was about 30 years old when He began His public ministry.

One day John saw Jesus coming toward him and said, "Look! This is the Lamb of God who takes away the world's sin! This is the one I was talking about when I said, 'Soon a man far greater than I am is coming who existed long before me!' I didn't know He was the one, but I am here baptizing with water in order to point Him out to the nation of Israel."

Then John told about seeing the Holy Spirit in the form of a dove descending from heaven and resting upon Jesus. "I didn't know He was the one," John said again, "but at the time God sent me to baptize, He told me, 'When you see the Holy Spirit descending and resting upon someone—He is the one you are looking for. He is the one who baptizes with the Holy Spirit.' I saw it happen to this man, and I therefore testify that He is the Son of God."

The following day as John was standing with two of his disciples, Jesus walked by. John looked at Him intently and then declared, "See! There is the Lamb of God!" Then two of John's disciples turned

Luke 3:23; John 1:29-37

and followed Jesus! Jesus looked around and saw them following. "What do you want?" He asked them.

"Sir," they replied, "where do You live?"

"Come and see," He said. So they went with Him to the place where He was staying and were with Him from about four o'clock that afternoon until the evening. One of these men was Andrew, Simon Peter's brother.

Andrew then went to find his brother Peter and told him, "We have found the Messiah!" And he brought him to Jesus.

Jesus looked intently at Peter for a moment and then said, "You are Simon, John's son—but you shall be called Peter, the Rock!"

The next day Jesus decided to go to Galilee. He found Philip and told him, "Come with Me." Philip was from Bethsaida, Andrew and Peter's home town.

Then Philip went off to look for Nathanael and told him, "We have found the Messiah!—the very person Moses and the prophets told about! His name is Jesus, the son of Joseph from Nazareth!"

"Nazareth!" exclaimed Nathanael, "Can anything good come from there?"

"Just come and see for yourself," Philip declared.

As they approached, Jesus said, "Here comes an honest man—a true son of Israel!"

"How do you know what I am like?" Nathanael demanded.

And Jesus replied, "I could see you under that fig

John 1:37-48

tree before Philip found you!"

Nathanael replied, "Sir, You are the Son of God —the King of Israel!"

Jesus asked him, "Do you believe all this just because I told you I had seen you under the fig tree? You will see greater proofs than this! You will even see heaven open and the angels of God coming back and forth to Me, the Son of Man."

March, A.D. 27

Two days later Jesus' mother was a guest at a wedding in the village of Cana in Galilee, and Jesus and His disciples were invited too. The wine supply ran out during the festivities, and Jesus' mother came to Him with the problem.

"I can't help you now," He said. "It isn't yet time for showing who I am."

Then His mother told the servants, "Do whatever He tells you!"

Six stone waterpots were standing there; they were used for Jewish ceremonial purposes and held perhaps 20 to 30 gallons each. Jesus told the servants to fill them to the brim with water. When this was done He said, "Dip some out and take it to the master of ceremonies."

When the master of ceremonies tasted the water that was now wine, not knowing where it had come from, though of course the servants did, he called the bridegroom over. "This is wonderful stuff!" he

John 1:48-51; John 2:1-10

said. "You're different from most hosts! Usually they give out the best wine first; and afterwards when everyone is full and doesn't care, then they bring out the less expensive brands! But you have kept the best for the last!"

This miracle at Cana in Galilee was Jesus' first demonstration of His heaven-sent power. And His disciples believed that He really was the Messiah.

After the wedding He left for Capernaum for a few days with His mother, brothers, and disciples.

John 2:10-12

So many people were
coming and going
that they
scarcely had time to eat.

PART 2

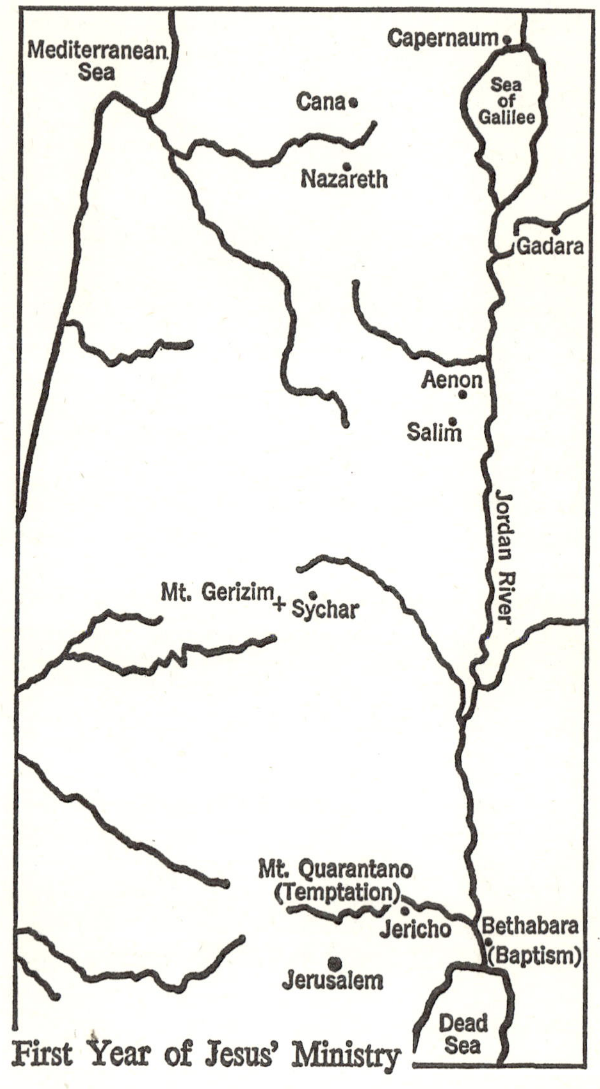

First Year of Jesus' Ministry

Chapter 7

First Clash

April or May, A.D. 27

It was time for the Jewish Passover celebration, and Jesus went to Jerusalem. In the Temple area He saw merchants selling cattle, sheep, and doves for sacrifices, and money changers behind their counters. Jesus made a whip from some ropes and chased them all out, and drove out the sheep and oxen, scattered the money changers' coins over the floor and turned over their tables! Then going over to the men selling doves, He told them, "Get these things out of here! Don't turn My Father's House into a market!"

Then His disciples remembered this Old Testament prophecy: "Concern for God's House will be My undoing!"

"What right have You to order them out?" the Jewish leaders demanded. "If You have this authority from God, show us a miracle to prove it."

"All right," Jesus replied, "this is the miracle I will do for you: Destroy this Sanctuary and in three days I will raise it up!"

"What!" they exclaimed. "It took 46 years to build this Temple, and You can do it in three days?"

John 2:13-20

But by "this Sanctuary" He meant His body. After He came back to life again, the disciples remembered His saying this and realized that what He had quoted from the Old Testament really did refer to Him and had come true!

Because of the miracles He did in Jerusalem at the Passover celebration, many people were convinced that He was indeed the Messiah. But Jesus didn't trust them, for He knew mankind to the core. No one needed to tell Him how changeable human beings are.

After dark one night a Jewish religious leader named Nicodemus, a member of the sect of the Pharisees, came for an interview with Jesus. "Sir," he said, "we all know that God has sent You to teach us. Your miracles are proof enough of this."

Jesus replied, "With all the earnestness I possess I tell you this: Unless you are born again, you can never get into the Kingdom of God."

"Born again!" exclaimed Nicodemus. "What do You mean? How can an old man go back into his mother's womb and be born again?"

Jesus replied, "What I am telling you so earnestly is this: Unless one is born of water and the Spirit, he cannot enter the Kingdom of God. Men can only reproduce human life, but the Holy Spirit gives you new life from heaven, so don't be surprised at My statement that you must be born again! Just as you can hear the wind but can't tell where it comes from or where it will go next, so it is with the Spirit! We

John 2:21-25; John 3:1-8

do not know on whom He will next bestow this life from heaven."

"What do You mean?" Nicodemus asked.

Jesus replied, "You, a respected Jewish teacher, and yet you don't understand these things? I am telling you what I know and have seen—and yet you won't believe Me. But if you don't even believe Me when I tell you about such things as these happening here among men, how can you possibly believe if I tell you what is going on in heaven? For only I, the Son of Man, have come to earth and will return to heaven again.

"And as Moses in the wilderness lifted up the image of a bronze serpent on a pole, even so must I be lifted up upon a pole so that anyone who believes in Me will have eternal life. For God loved the world so much that He gave His only Son so that anyone who believes in Him will not perish but have eternal life.

"God did not send His Son into the world to condemn the world, but to save it. There is no eternal doom awaiting those who are trusting Him to save them. But those who don't trust Him have already been tried and condemned for not believing in the only Son of God. Their sentence is based on this fact: That the Light from heaven came into the world, but they loved their former darkness more than the Light, for their deeds were evil. They hated the heavenly Light because they wanted to

John 3:8-20

sin in the darkness. They stayed away from that Light for fear their sins would be exposed and they would be punished. But those doing right come gladly to the Light to let everyone see that they are doing what God wants them to."

Summer—Fall, A.D. 27

Afterwards Jesus and His disciples left Jerusalem and stayed for a while in Judea and baptized people there.

John the Baptist was not yet in prison. He was baptizing at Aenon, near Salim, because there was plenty of water there.

One day someone began an argument with John's disciples, telling them that Jesus' baptism was best. So they came to John and said, "Master, the man you met on the other side of the Jordan River—the one you said was the Messiah—He is baptizing too, and everybody is going over there instead of coming here to us."

John replied, "God in heaven appoints each man's work. My work is to prepare the way for that man so that everyone will go to Him. You yourselves know how plainly I told you that I am not the Messiah. I am here to prepare the way before Him—that is all.

"The crowds will naturally go to the main attraction—the bride will go where the bridegroom is! A bridegroom's friends rejoice with him. I am the

John 3:20-29

bridegroom's friend, and I am filled with joy at His success. He must become greater and greater, and I must become less and less. He has come from heaven and is greater than anyone else. I am of the earth, and my understanding is limited to the things of earth.

"He tells what He has seen and heard, but how few believe what He tells them! Those who believe Him discover that God is a fountain of truth! For this one—sent by God—speaks God's words, for God's Spirit is upon Him without measure or limit. The Father loves this man because He is His Son, and God has given Him everything there is. And all who trust Him—God's Son—to save them have eternal life; those who don't believe and obey Him shall never see heaven, but the wrath of God remains upon them."

After John had publicly criticized Herod, governor of Galilee, for marrying Herodias, his brother's wife, and for many other wrongs he had done, Herod put John in prison, thus adding this sin to all his many others.

John 3:29-36; Luke 3:19, 20

Chapter 8

Strange Encounter

January, A.D. 28

When Jesus heard that John had been arrested, He left Judea and returned home to Nazareth in Galilee. He had to go through Samaria on the way.

Around noon as He approached the village of Sychar, He came to Jacob's Well, located on the parcel of ground Jacob gave to his son Joseph. Jesus was tired from the long walk in the hot sun and sat wearily beside the well. Soon a Samaritan woman came to draw water, and Jesus asked her for a drink. He was alone at the time as His disciples had gone into the village to buy some food. The woman was surprised that a Jew would ask a "despised Samaritan" for anything, usually they didn't even speak to them, and she remarked about this to Jesus.

He replied, "If you only knew what a wonderful gift God has for you, and who I am, you would ask Me for some living water!"

"But You don't have a rope or a bucket," she said, "and this is a very deep well! From where would you get this living water? And besides, are you greater than our ancestor Jacob? How can you offer better water than this which he himself enjoyed, along with his sons and cattle?"

Matthew 4:12; John 4:4-12

Jesus replied that people soon became thirsty again after drinking that water. "But the water I give them," He said, "becomes a perpetual spring within them, watering them forever with eternal life."

"Please, Sir," the woman said, "give me some of that water! Then I'll never be thirsty again and won't have to make this long trip out here every day."

"Go and get your husband," Jesus told her.

"But I'm not married," the woman replied.

"All too true!" Jesus said, "for you have had five husbands, and you aren't even married to the man you're living with now! You couldn't have spoken a truer word!"

"Sir," the woman said, "You must be a prophet! But say, tell me, why is it you Jews insist that Jerusalem is the only place of worship, while we Samaritans claim it is here at Mount Gerazim, where our ancestors worshiped?"

Jesus replied, "The time is coming, Ma'am, when we will no longer be concerned about whether to worship the Father here or in Jerusalem! For it's not *where* we worship that counts, but *how* we worship—is our worship spiritual and real? Do we have the Holy Spirit's help? For God is Spirit, and we must have His Spirit's help to worship as we should. The Father wants this kind of worship from us. But you Samaritans know so little about Him, worshiping blindly, while we Jews know all about

John 4:12-24

Him, for salvation comes to the world through the Jews."

The woman said, "Well, at least I know that the Messiah will come—the one they call Christ—and when He does, He will explain everything to us."

Then Jesus told her, "I am the Messiah!"

Just then His disciples arrived. They were surprised to find Him talking to a woman, but none of them asked Him why, or what they had been discussing.

Then the woman left her waterpot beside the well and went back to the village and told everyone, "Come and meet a man who told me everything I ever did! Can this be the Messiah?" So the people came streaming from the village to see Him.

Meanwhile, the disciples were urging Jesus to eat. "No," He said, "I have some food you don't know about!"

"Who brought it to Him?" the disciples asked one another.

Then Jesus explained: "My nourishment comes from doing the will of God who sent Me and finishing His work. Do you think the work of harvesting will not begin until the summer ends four months from now? Look around you! Vast fields of human souls are ripening all around us and are ready now for reaping. The reapers will be paid good wages and will be gathering eternal souls into the granaries of heaven! What joys await the sower and the reaper, both together! For it is true that

John 4:22,25-37

one sows and someone else reaps. I sent you to reap where you didn't sow; others did the work, and you received the harvest!"

Many from that Samaritan village believed He was the Messiah because of the woman's report, "He told me everything I ever did!" So when they saw Him at the well, they begged Him to stay at their village; and He did for two days.

While He was there teaching them, many others believed. Then they said to the woman, "Now we believe because we have heard Him ourselves, not just because of what you told us. He is indeed the Savior of the world."

At the end of the two days' stay He went on into Galilee. For as Jesus used to say, "A prophet is honored everywhere but in his own country!" And sure enough, the Galileans welcomed Him with open arms, for they had been in Jerusalem at the Passover celebration and had seen some of His miracles. He became well known throughout all that region for His sermons in the synagogues; everyone praised Him.

John 4:37-45; Luke 4:14,15

Chapter 9

Back Home

Before April, A.D. 28

In the course of His journey through Galilee He arrived at the town of Cana, where He had turned the water into wine. While He was there, a government official in the city of Capernaum, whose son was very sick, heard that Jesus had come from Judea and was traveling in Galilee. This man went over to Cana, found Jesus, and begged Him to come to Capernaum with him and heal his son, who was now at death's door.

Jesus asked, "Won't any of you believe in Me unless I do more and more miracles?"

The official pled, "Sir, please come now before my child dies."

Then Jesus told him, "Go back home. Your son is healed!" And the man believed Jesus and started home.

While he was on his way, some of his servants met him with the news that all was well—his son had recovered! He asked them when the lad had begun to feel better, and they replied, "Yesterday afternoon at about one o'clock when his fever was suddenly gone!" Then the father realized it was the same moment that Jesus had told him, "Your son is

John 4:46-53

healed." And the officer and his entire household believed that Jesus was the Messiah.

This was Jesus' second miracle in Galilee after coming from Judea.

When He came to the village of Nazareth, His boyhood home, He went, as usual, to the synagogue on Saturday, and stood up to read the Scriptures. The book of Isaiah the prophet was handed to Him, and He opened it to the place where it says: "The Spirit of the Lord is upon Me; He has appointed Me to preach Good News to the poor; He has sent Me to announce that captives shall be released and the blind shall see, that the downtrodden shall be freed from their oppressors, and that God is ready to give blessings to all who come to Him."

Then He closed the book and handed it back to the attendant and sat down, while everyone in the synagogue gazed at Him intently. Then He added, "These Scriptures came true today!"

All who were there spoke well of Him and were amazed by the beautiful words that fell from His lips. "How can this be?" they asked. "Isn't this Joseph's son?"

Then He said, "Probably you will quote Me that proverb, 'Physician, heal Yourself'—meaning, 'Why don't You do miracles here in Your home town as you did in Capernaum?' But I solemnly declare to you that no prophet is accepted in his own home town! For example, remember how Elijah, the prophet, used a miracle to help the widow of Zare-

John 4:53,54; Luke 4:16-25

phath—a foreigner from the land of Sidon. There were many Jewish widows needing help in those days of famine, for there had been no rain for three and one-half years and hunger stalked the land; yet Elijah was not sent to them. Or think of the prophet Elisha, who healed Naaman, a Syrian, rather than the many Jewish lepers needing his help."

As He made these remarks, the people in the synagogue were filled with sudden fury; and jumping up, they mobbed Him and took Him to the edge of the hill on which the city was built, to push Him over the cliff. But He walked away through the crowd and left them.

Soon He moved to Capernaum, beside the Lake of Galilee, close to Zebulon and Naphtali. This fulfilled Isaiah's prophecy: "The land of Zebulon and the land of Naphtali, beside the Lake, and the countryside beyond the Jordan River, and Upper Galilee where so many foreigners live have become places of glory. The people who sat in darkness have seen a great Light; they sat in the land of death, and the Light broke through upon them."

From then on, Jesus began to preach, "At last the time has come!" He announced. "God's Kingdom is near! Turn from your sins and act on this glorious news!"

One day as He was preaching on the shore of Lake Gennesaret, great crowds pressed in on Him to listen to the Word of God. He noticed two empty boats standing at the water's edge, while the fisher-

Luke 4:25-30; Matthew 4:13-17; Mark 1:15; Luke 5:1,2

men washed their nets. Stepping into one of the boats, Jesus asked Simon (its owner) to push out a little into the water, so that He could sit in the boat and speak to the crowds from there. When He had finished speaking, He said to Simon, "Now go out where it is deeper and let down your nets and you will catch a lot of fish!"

"Sir," Simon replied, "we worked hard all last night and didn't catch a thing! But if You say so, we'll try again."

And this time their nets were so full that they began to tear! A shout for help brought their partners in the other boat, and soon both boats were filled with fish and on the verge of sinking!

When Simon Peter realized what had happened, he fell to his knees before Jesus and said, "Oh, Sir, please leave us, for I'm too much of a sinner for You to be around." For he was awestruck by the size of their catch, as were the others with him, and his partners too—James and John, the sons of Zebedee.

Jesus replied, "Don't worry! Come along with Me and I will show you how to fish for the souls of men!"

And as soon as they landed, they left everything and went with Him.

Jesus and His companions soon arrived at the town of Capernaum and on Saturday morning went into the Jewish place of worship—the synagogue—where He preached. The congregation was sur-

Luke 5:2-10; Matthew 4:19; Luke 5:11; Mark 1:21

prised at His sermon because He spoke as an authority, and didn't try to prove His points by quoting others—quite unlike what they were used to hearing!

Mark 1:21,22

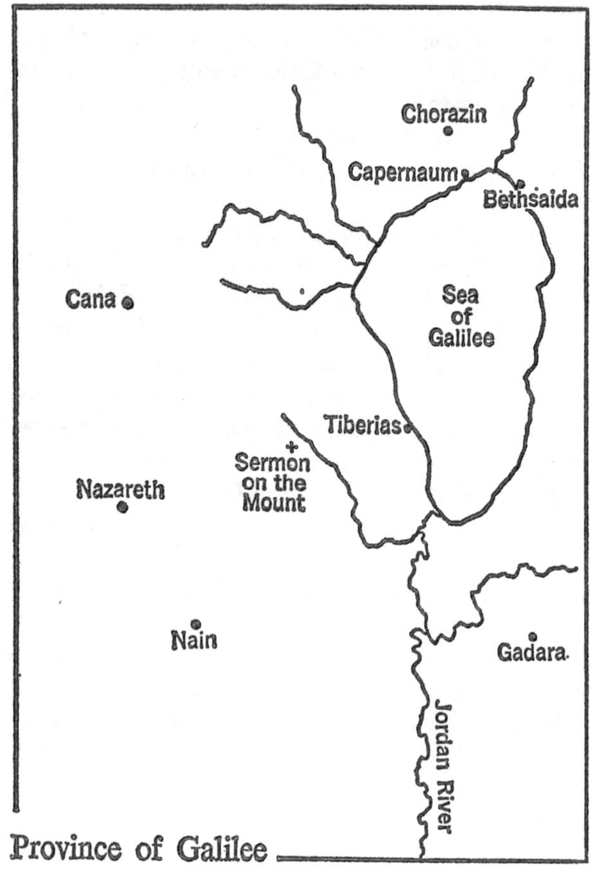

Province of Galilee

Chapter 10

Help for Unknowns

Once as He was teaching in the synagogue, a man possessed by a demon began shouting at Jesus, "Go away! We want nothing to do with You, Jesus of Nazareth. You have come to destroy us! I know who You are—the Holy Son of God!"

Jesus cut him short. "Be silent!" He told the demon. "Come out!" The demon threw the man to the floor as the crowd watched, and then left him without hurting him further.

Amazed, the people asked, "What is in this man's words that even demons obey Him?" The story of what He had done spread like wildfire throughout the whole region.

After leaving the synagogue that day, He went to Simon's home where He found Simon's mother-in-law very sick with a high fever. "Please heal her," everyone begged. Standing at her bedside, He spoke to the fever, rebuking it, and immediately her temperature returned to normal and she got up and prepared a meal for them!

As the sun went down that evening, all the villagers who had sick people in their homes, no matter what their diseases were, brought them to Jesus; and the touch of His hands healed everyone! Some were possessed by demons; and the demons

Luke 4:33-41

came out at His command, shouting, "You are the Son of God!" But He stopped them and told them to be silent, because they knew He was the Christ.

One morning He was up long before daybreak, and went out alone into the wilderness to pray. Later, Simon and the others went out searching for Him and told Him, "Everyone is asking for You."

But He replied, "We must go on to other towns as well, give them My message, too, for that is why I came."

So He traveled throughout the province of Galilee, preaching in the synagogues and releasing many from the power of demons. The report of His miracles spread far beyond the borders of Galilee, so that sick folk were soon coming to be healed from as far away as Syria. They had every kind of illness and pain, or were possessed by demons, or were insane, or paralyzed—and He healed them all. Enormous crowds followed Him wherever He went—people from Galilee, and the Ten Cities, and Jerusalem, and from all over Judea, and even from across the Jordan River.

One day when He was in a certain village, a man with an advanced case of leprosy was there. When he saw Jesus he fell to the ground before Him, face downward in the dust, begging to be healed. "Sir," he said, "if You only will, You can clear me of every trace of my disease."

Jesus reached out and touched the man and said,

Luke 4:41; Mark 1:35-39; Matthew 4:24,25; Luke 5:12,13

"Of course I will! Be healed!" And immediately the leprosy was gone—the man was healed!

Jesus then told him sternly, "Go and be examined immediately by the Jewish priest. Don't stop to speak to anyone along the way. Take along the offering prescribed by Moses for a leper who is healed, so that everyone will have proof that you are well again." But as the man went on his way he began to shout the good news that he was healed; as a result, such throngs soon surrounded Jesus that He couldn't publicly enter a city anywhere, but had to stay out in the barren wastelands. And people from everywhere came to Him there. But He often withdrew to the wilderness for prayer.

Several days later He returned to Capernaum, and the news of His arrival spread quickly through the city. Soon the house where He was staying was so packed with visitors that there wasn't room for a single person more, not even outside the door. And He preached the Word to them.

Then—look! Four men came carrying a paralyzed man on a sleeping mat. They tried to push through the crowd to Jesus but couldn't reach Him. So they went up on the roof above Him, took off some tiles and lowered the sick man down into the middle of the crowd, still on his sleeping mat, right in front of Jesus! Seeing their faith, Jesus said to the man, "My friend, your sins are forgiven!"

"Who does this fellow think He is?" the Pharisees and teachers of the Law exclaimed among them-

Mark 1:42-45; Luke 5:16; Mark 2:1-3; Luke 5:18-21

selves. "This is blasphemy! Who but God can forgive sins?"

Jesus knew what they were thinking, and He replied, "Why is it blasphemy? Which is easier for Me to do, to say I have forgiven his sins, or to actually heal him? Now I will prove My authority to forgive sin by demonstrating My power to heal disease." Then He said to the paralyzed man, "Get up, roll up your sleeping mat and go on home!"

So he jumped up and left!

A chill of fear swept through the crowd when they saw it happen, then how they praised God! "We've never seen anything like this before!" they all exclaimed.

Jesus went out to the seashore again, and preached to the crowds that gathered around Him. As He was walking up the beach He saw Levi, the son of Alphaeus, sitting at his tax collection booth. "Come with Me," Jesus told him. "Come be My disciple!" So Levi left everything, sprang up and went with Him!

Soon Levi held a reception in his home, with Jesus as the guest of honor. Many of Levi's fellow tax collectors and other guests were there. But the Pharisees and teachers of the Law complained bitterly to Jesus' disciples about His eating with such notorious sinners. Jesus answered them, "It is the sick who need a doctor, not those in good health! My purpose is to invite sinners to turn from their

Luke 5:21-24; Matthew 9:7,8; Mark 2:12-14; Luke 5:28-32

sins, not to spend My time with those who think themselves already good enough."

One day the disciples of John the Baptist came to Jesus and asked Him, "Why don't your disciples fast, going without food at times to honor God? We do it regularly and so do the Pharisees!"

Jesus asked, "Do happy men fast? Do wedding guests go hungry while celebrating with the groom? But the time will come when the bridegroom will be killed; then they won't want to eat!"

Then Jesus told them a story: "No one tears up unshrunk cloth to make patches for old clothes, for the new garment is ruined and the old one isn't helped when the patch tears out again! And no one puts new wine into old wineskins, for the new wine bursts the old skins, ruining the skins and spilling the wine! New wine must be put into new wineskins. But no one after drinking the old wine seems to want the fresh and the new! 'The old ways are best,' they say."

Luke 5:32; Matthew 9:14; Luke 5:34-39

Chapter 11

Break with Tradition

April, A.D. 28

Afterwards Jesus returned to Jerusalem for one of the Jewish religious holidays. Inside the city near the Sheep Gate was Bethesda Pool, with five covered platforms or porches surrounding it. Crowds of sick folks—lame, blind, or with paralyzed limbs—lay on the platforms waiting for a certain movement of the water, for an angel of the Lord came from time to time and disturbed the water, and the first person to step down into it afterwards was healed!

One of the men lying there had been sick for 38 years. When Jesus saw him and knew how long he had been ill, He asked him, "Would you like to get well?"

"I can't," the sick man said, "for I have no one to help me into the pool at the movement of the water. While I am trying to get there, someone else always gets in ahead of me."

Jesus told him, "Stand up, roll up your sleeping mat and go on home!"

Instantly, the man was healed! He rolled up the mat and began walking! But it was on the Sabbath when this miracle was done. So the Jewish leaders

John 5:1-10

objected! They said to the man who was cured, "You can't work on the Sabbath! It's illegal to carry that sleeping mat!"

"The man who healed me told me to," was his reply.

"Who said such a thing as that?" they demanded.

The man didn't know, and Jesus had disappeared into the crowd. But afterwards Jesus found him in the Temple and told him, "Now you are well; don't sin as you did before, or something even worse may happen to you."

Then the man went to find the Jewish leaders, and told them it was Jesus who had healed him. So they began harassing Jesus as a Sabbath breaker. But Jesus replied, "My Father constantly does good, and I'm following His example!"

Then the Jewish leaders were all the more eager to kill Him because in addition to disobeying their Sabbath laws, He had spoken of God as His Father, thereby making Himself equal with God.

Jesus replied, "The Son can do nothing by Himself. He does only what He sees the Father doing, and in the same way. For the Father loves the Son, and tells Him everything He is doing; and the Son will do far more awesome miracles than this man's healing! He will even raise from the dead anyone He wants to, just as the Father does. And the Father leaves all judgment of sin to His Son, so that everyone will honor the Son, just as they honor the Father. But if you refuse to honor God's Son, whom

John 5:10-23

He sent to you, then you are certainly not honoring the Father.

"I say emphatically that anyone who listens to My message and believes in God who sent Me has eternal life, and will never be damned for his sins, but has already passed out of death into life. And I solemnly declare that the time is coming, in fact, it is here, when the dead shall hear My voice—the voice of the Son of God—and those who listen shall live. The Father has life in Himself, and has granted His Son to have life in Himself, and to judge the sins of all mankind because He is the Son of Man.

"Don't be so surprised! Indeed the time is coming when all the dead in their graves shall hear the voice of God's Son and shall rise again—those who have done good, to eternal life; and those who have continued in evil, to judgment.

"But I pass no judgment without consulting the Father. I judge as I am told. And My judgment is absolutely fair and just, for it is according to the will of God who sent Me and is not merely My own! When I make claims about Myself they aren't believed, but someone else, yes, John the Baptist, is making these claims for Me. You have gone out to listen to his preaching, and I know that all he says about Me is true!

"But the truest witness I have is not from a man, though I have reminded you about John's witness so that you will believe in Me and be saved. John

John 5:23-35

shone brightly for a while, and you benefited and rejoiced, but I have a greater witness than John. I refer to the miracles I do; these have been assigned Me by the Father, and they prove that the Father has sent Me. And the Father Himself has also testified about Me, though not appearing to you personally, or speaking to you directly. But you are not listening to Him, for you refuse to believe Me—the one sent to you with God's message.

"You search the Scriptures, for you believe they give you eternal life. And the Scriptures point to Me! Yet you won't come to Me so that I can give you this life eternal! Your approval or disapproval means nothing to Me, for as I know so well, you don't have God's love within you. I know because I have come to you representing My Father and you refuse to welcome Me, though you readily enough receive those who aren't sent from Him, but represent only themselves! No wonder you can't believe! For you gladly honor each other, but you don't care about the honor that comes from the only God!

"Yet it is not I who will accuse you of this to the Father—Moses will! Moses, on whose laws you set your hopes of heaven. For you have refused to believe Moses. He wrote about Me, but you refuse to believe him, so you refuse to believe in Me. And since you don't believe what he wrote, no wonder you don't believe Me either."

John 5:35-47

May, A.D. 28

Another time, on a Sabbath day, as Jesus and His disciples were walking through the fields, the disciples were breaking off heads of wheat and eating the grain. Some of the Jewish religious leaders said to Jesus, "They shouldn't be doing that! It's against our laws to harvest grain on the Sabbath."

But Jesus replied, "Didn't you ever hear about the time David and his companions were hungry, and he went into the house of God—Abiathar was high priest then—and they ate the special bread only priests were allowed to eat? That was against the law too. But the Sabbath was made to benefit man, and not man to benefit the Sabbath.

"And haven't you ever read in the Old Testament how the priests on duty in the Temple may work on the Sabbath? And truly, One is here who is greater than the Temple! But if you had known the meaning of this Scripture verse, 'I want you to be merciful more than I want your offerings,' you would not have condemned those who aren't guilty! For I, the Son of Man, am master even of the Sabbath."

On another Sabbath He was in the synagogue teaching, and a man was present whose right hand was deformed. The teachers of the Law and the Pharisees watched closely to see whether He would heal the man that day, since it was the Sabbath! For they were eager to find some charge to bring

Mark 2:23-26; Matthew 12:5-8; Luke 6:6,7

against Him. How well He knew their thoughts! But He said to the man with the deformed hand, "Come and stand here where everyone can see." So he did.

Then Jesus said to the Pharisees and teachers of the Law, "I have a question for you. Is it right to do good on the Sabbath day, or to do harm? To save life, or to destroy it? If you had just one sheep, and it fell into a well on the Sabbath, would you work to rescue it that day? Of course you would! And how much more valuable is a person than a sheep! Yes, it is right to do good on the Sabbath!"

Then He said to the man, "Stretch out your arm!" And as he did, his hand became normal, just like the other one!

Then the Pharisees went away to plot Jesus' arrest and death.

Luke 6:7-9; Matthew 12:11-14

Chapter 12

Some Revolutionary Ideas

Summer, A.D. 28

Jesus and His disciples withdrew to the beach, followed by a huge crowd from all over Galilee, Judea, Jerusalem, Idumea, from beyond the Jordan River and even from as far away as Tyre and Sidon. For the news about His miracles had spread far and wide and vast numbers came to see Him for themselves.

He instructed His disciples to bring around a boat and have it standing ready to rescue Him in case He was crowded off the beach. For He had healed many that day, and as a result, great numbers of sick people were crowding around Him, trying to touch Him. And whenever those possessed by demons caught sight of Him, they would fall down before Him, shrieking out, "You are the Son of God!" But He strictly warned them not to make Him known.

One day soon afterwards He went out into the mountains to pray, and prayed all night. At daybreak He called together His followers and chose twelve of them to be the inner circle of His disciples. They were appointed as His "apostles," or, "missionaries." Here are their names:

Mark 3:7-12; Luke 6:12,13

Simon, He also called him Peter,
Andrew, Simon's brother,
James,
John,
Philip,
Bartholomew,
Matthew,
Thomas,
James the son of Alphaeus,
Simon also called "Zealotes,"
Judas son of James,
Judas Iscariot who later betrayed Him.

One day as the crowds were gathering, He went up the hillside with His disciples, and sat down and taught them there.

"Humble men are very fortunate!" He told them, "for the Kingdom of Heaven is given to them!

"Those who mourn are fortunate! For they shall be comforted!

"The meek and lowly are fortunate! For the whole wide world belongs to them!

"Happy are those who long for justice, for they shall surely have it.

"Happy are the kind and merciful, for they shall be shown mercy.

"Happy are those whose hearts are pure, for they shall see God!

"Happy are those who strive for peace—they shall be called the sons of God!

"Happy are those who are persecuted because

Luke 6:13-16; Matthew 5:1-10

they are good, for the Kingdom of Heaven is theirs! What happiness it is when others hate you and exclude you and insult you and smear your name because you are Mine! When you are reviled and persecuted and lied about because you are My followers—wonderful! When that happens, rejoice! Yes, jump for joy! For you will have a great reward awaiting you in heaven! And you will be in good company—the ancient prophets were treated that way too!

"But, oh, the sorrows that await the rich! For they have had their happiness down here. They are fat and prosperous now, but a time of awful hunger is before them. Their careless laughter now, means sorrow then. And what sadness is ahead for those praised by the crowds—for false prophets have always been praised!

"You are the world's seasoning, to make it tolerable. If you lose your flavor, what will happen to the world? And you will be thrown away and trampled underfoot as valueless.

"You are the world's light—a city on a hill, glowing in the night for all to see. Don't hide your light! Let it shine for all; let your good deeds glow for all men to see, so that they will praise your heavenly Father.

"Don't misunderstand why I have come—it isn't to cancel the Old Testament laws and the warnings of the prophets. No, I came to fulfill them, and to make them all come true. With all the earnestness I

Matthew 5:10; Luke 6:22; Matthew 5:11; Luke 6:23-26; Matthew 5:13-18

have I say, every law in the Book will continue until its purpose is achieved. And so if anyone breaks the least commandments, and teaches others to, he shall be the least in the Kingdom of Heaven. But those who teach God's laws, and obey them, shall be great in the Kingdom of Heaven. But I warn you—unless your goodness is greater than that of the Pharisees and other Jewish leaders, you can't get into the Kingdom of Heaven at all!

"Under the Old Testament laws the rule was, 'If you kill, you must die.' But I have added to that rule, and tell you that if you are only angry, even in your own home, you are in danger of judgment! If you call your friend an idiot, you are in danger of being brought before the court. And if you curse him, you are in danger of the fires of hell.

"So if you are standing before the altar in the Temple, offering a sacrifice to God, and suddenly remember that a friend has something against you, leave your sacrifice there beside the altar and go and apologize and be reconciled to him, and then come and offer your sacrifice to God. Come to terms quickly with your enemy, before it is too late, and he drags you into court and you are thrown into a debtor's cell. For you will stay there until you have paid the last penny.

"The Old Testament law said, 'You shall not commit adultery.' But I say, anyone who even looks at a woman with lust in his eye has already committed adultery with her in his heart.

Matthew 5:18-28

"So if your eye—even if it is your best eye!—causes you to lust, gouge it out and throw it away. Better for part of you to be destroyed than for all of you to be cast into hell. And if your hand—even your right hand!—causes you to sin, cut it off and throw it away. Better that than find yourself in hell.

"The Old Testament law said, 'If anyone wants to be rid of his wife, he can divorce her merely by giving her a letter of dismissal.' But I say that a man who divorces his wife, except for unfaithfulness, causes her to commit adultery. And if anyone marries her, he commits adultery.

"Again, the Old Testament law says, 'You shall not break your vows to God, but must fulfill them all.' But I say, don't make any vows! And even to say, 'By heavens,' is a sacred vow to God, for the heavens are God's throne! And if you say, 'By the earth,' it is a sacred vow, for the earth is His footstool! And don't swear, 'By Jerusalem' for this too is a sacred vow because Jerusalem is the capital of the great King. Don't even swear, 'By my head!' for you can't turn one hair white or black! Say just a simple 'Yes, I will' or 'No, I won't!' Your word is enough. To strengthen your promise with a vow shows that something is wrong.

"The Old Testament law said, 'If a man gouges out another's eye, he must pay with his own eye. If a tooth gets knocked out, knock out the tooth of the one who did it.' But I say, don't resist violence! If you are slapped on one cheek, turn the other too! If

Matthew 5:29-39

you are ordered to court, and your shirt is taken from you, give them your coat too. If the military compel you to carry their gear for a mile, carry it two. Give to those who ask from you, and don't turn away from those who want to borrow.

"There is a saying, 'Love your friends and hate your enemies!' But I say, Love your enemies! Pray for those who persecute you! In that way you will be acting as true sons of your Father in heaven. For He gives His sunlight to both the evil and the good, and sends rain on the just and on the unjust too. If you love only those who love you, what good is that? Even scoundrels do that much! If you are friendly only to your friends, how are you different from anyone else? Even the heathen do that!

"And if you only do good to those who do you good—is that so wonderful? Even sinners do that much! And if you only lend money to those whom you expect to repay you, what good is that? Even the most wicked will lend to their own kind for full return!

"No! Love your enemies! Do good to them! Lend to them! And don't be concerned about the fact that they won't repay! Then your reward from heaven will be very great, and you will truly be acting as sons of God: for He is kind to the unthankful and to those who are very wicked. Try to show as much compassion as your Father does.

"You are to be perfect, even as your Father in heaven is perfect!

Matthew 5:40-47; Luke 6:33-36; Matthew 5:48

"Take care! Don't do your good deeds publicly, to be admired, for then you will lose the reward from your Father in heaven. When you give a gift to a beggar, don't shout about it as the hypocrites do—blowing trumpets in the synagogues and streets to call attention to their acts of charity! I tell you in all earnestness, they have received all the reward they will ever get! But when you do a kindness to someone, do it secretly—don't tell your left hand what your right hand is doing! And when you do it secretly, your Father who knows all secrets will reward you.

"And now about prayer. When you pray, don't be like the hypocrites who pretend piety by praying publicly on street corners and in the synagogues where everyone can see them! Truly, that is all the reward they will ever get! But when you pray, go away by yourself, all alone, and shut the door behind you and pray to your Father secretly, and your Father, who knows your secrets, will reward you. Don't recite the same prayer over and over, as the heathen do, who think prayers are answered only by repeating them again and again. Remember, your Father knows exactly what you need even before you ask Him!

"Pray along these lines: 'Our Father in heaven, we honor Your holy name. We ask that Your kingdom will come soon. May Your will be done here on earth, just as it is in heaven. Give us our food again today, as usual, and forgive us our sins, just

Matthew 6:1-12

as we have forgiven those who have sinned against us. Don't bring us into temptation, but deliver us from the Evil One. For Yours is the kingdom and the power and the glory forever. Amen.'

"Your heavenly Father will forgive you if you forgive those who sin against you; but if you refuse to forgive them, He will not forgive you.

"And now about fasting. When you fast, declining your food for a spiritual purpose, don't do it publicly, as the hypocrites do, who try to look wan and disheveled so people will feel sorry for them! Truly, that is the only reward they will ever get! But when you fast, put on festive clothing, so that no one will suspect you are hungry, except your Father who knows every secret! And He will reward you!

"Don't store up your profits here on earth, where they erode away, and can be stolen! But store them in heaven, where they never lose their value, and are safe from thieves! If your profits are in heaven your heart will be there too!

"If your eye is pure, there will be sunshine in your soul. But if your eye is clouded with evil thoughts and desires, you are in deep spiritual darkness. And oh how deep that darkness can be! You cannot serve two masters: God and money. For you will hate one and love the other, or else the other way around.

"So my counsel is, don't worry about things—food, drink, and clothes. For you already have life

Matthew 6:12-25

and a body—and they are far more important than what to eat and wear. Look at the birds! They don't worry about what to eat—they don't sow or reap or store up food—and your heavenly Father feeds them. And you are far more valuable to Him than they are! Will all your worries add a single moment to your life?

"And why worry about your clothes? Look at the field lilies! They don't worry about theirs! Yet King Solomon in all his glory was not clothed as beautifully as they! And if God cares so wonderfully for flowers that are here today and gone tomorrow, won't He more surely care for you, O men of little faith? So don't worry at all about having enough food and clothing.

"Don't be like the heathen! They take pride in these things, and are deeply concerned about them. But your heavenly Father already knows perfectly well that you need them. And He will give them to you gladly if you put Him first in your life. So don't be anxious about tomorrow! God will take care of your tomorrow too! Live one day at a time.

"Never criticize or condemn—or it will all come back on you! Go easy on others; then they will do the same for you! For if you give, you will get! Your gift will return to you in full and overflowing measure, pressed down, shaken together to make room for more, and running over. Whatever measure you use to give—large or small—will be used to measure what is given back to you.

Matthew 6:25-34; Luke 6:37,38

"What good is it for one blind man to lead another? He will fall into a ditch and pull the other down with him. How can a student know more than his teacher? But if he works hard, he may learn as much.

"And why quibble about the speck in someone else's eye—his little fault—when a board is in your own? How can you think of saying to him, 'Brother, let me help you get rid of that speck in your eye,' when you can't see past the board in yours? Hypocrite! First get rid of the board, and then perhaps you can see well enough to deal with his speck!

"Don't give holy things to depraved men! Don't give pearls to swine! They will trample the pearls and turn and attack you.

"Ask, and you will be given what you ask for! Seek, and you will find! Knock, and the door will be opened! For everyone who asks, receives. Anyone who seeks, finds. If only you will knock, the door will open.

"If a child asks his father for a loaf of bread, will he be given a stone instead? If he asks for fish, will he be given a poisonous snake? Of course not! And if you hardhearted, sinful men know how to give good gifts to your children, won't your Father in heaven even more certainly give good gifts to those who ask Him for them?

"Do for others what you want them to do for you. This is the teaching of the Old Testament in a nutshell.

Luke 6:39-42; Matthew 7:6-12

"Heaven can be entered only through the narrow gate! The highway to hell is broad, and its gate is wide enough for all the multitudes who choose its easy way. But the Gateway to Life is small, and the road is narrow, and only a few ever find it.

"Beware of false teachers, who come disguised as harmless sheep but are wolves and will tear you apart. You can detect them by the way they act, just as you can identify a tree by its fruit. You need never confuse grapevines with thorn bushes! Or figs with thistles! Different kinds of fruit trees can quickly be identified by examining their fruit. For a variety producing delicious fruit doesn't produce a kind that is inedible! And a tree producing an inedible variety can't produce what is good! So the trees having the inedible fruit are chopped down and thrown on the fire. Yes, the way to identify a tree, or a person, is by the kind of fruit produced.

"Not all who talk like godly people are. They may refer to Me as 'Lord,' but still won't get to heaven. For the decisive question is whether they obey My Father in heaven. At the Judgment many will tell me, 'Lord, Lord, we told others about You, and used Your name to cast out demons, and to do many other great miracles.' But I will reply, 'You have never been Mine. Go away, for your deeds are evil.'

"All who listen to My instructions and follow them are wise, like a man who builds his house on solid rock. Though the rain comes in torrents, and the floods rise and the storm winds beat against his house, it won't collapse, for it is built on rock.

"But those who hear My instructions and ignore them are foolish, like a man who builds his house on sand. For when the rains and floods come, and storm winds beat against his house, it will fall with a mighty crash."

Large crowds followed Jesus as He came down the hillside. They were amazed at His sermons, for He taught as one who had great authority, and not as their Jewish leaders.

Matthew 7:25-27; Matthew 8:1; Matthew 7:28,29

Chapter 13

Without Prejudice

When Jesus arrived in Capernaum, a Roman army captain came and pled with Him to come to his home and heal his servant boy who was in bed paralyzed and racked with pain. Some respected Jewish elders began pleading earnestly with Jesus to come with them and help the man. They told Him what a wonderful person the captain was. "If anyone deserves Your help, it is he," they said, "for he loves the Jews and even paid personally for building us a synagogue!"

"Yes," Jesus said, "I will come and heal him."

Then the officer said, "Sir, I am not worthy to have You in my home; and it isn't necessary for You to come. If right here You will just say, 'Be healed,' my servant will get well! I know, because I am under the authority of my superior officers, and I have authority over my soldiers, and I say to one, 'Go,' and he goes, and to another, 'Come,' and he comes, and to my slave boy, 'Do this or that,' and he does it. And I know You have authority to tell his sickness to go—and it will go!"

Jesus stood there amazed! Turning to the crowd following Him, He said, "I haven't seen faith like this in all the land of Israel! And I tell you this, that many Gentiles like this Roman officer, shall come

Matthew 8:5,6; Luke 7:3-5; Matthew 8:7-11

from all over the world and sit down in the Kingdom of Heaven with Abraham, Isaac, and Jacob. And many an Israelite—those for whom the kingdom was prepared—shall be cast into outer darkness, to the place of weeping and torment."

Then Jesus said to the Roman officer, "Go on home. What you have believed has happened!" And the boy was healed that same hour!

Not long afterwards Jesus went with His disciples to the village of Nain, with the usual vast crowd at His heels. As He approached the village gate, a funeral procession was coming out. The boy who had died was the only son of his widowed mother, and following along with her were many mourners from the village.

When the Lord saw her, His heart overflowed with sympathy. "Don't cry!" He said. Then, as He walked over to the coffin and touched it, the bearers stopped. And He said, "Laddie, come back to life again!" The boy sat up and began to talk to those around him! And Jesus gave him back to his mother.

Then a great fear swept the crowd, and they exclaimed with praises to God, "A mighty prophet has risen among us," and, "We have seen the hand of God at work today." The report of what He did that morning raced from end to end of Judea and out across the borders into the surrounding country.

When John, in prison, heard about all the miracles the Messiah was doing, he sent two of his

Matthew 8:11-13; Luke 7:11-17; Matthew 11:2; Luke 7:19

disciples to ask Jesus, "Are You really the One we are waiting for, or shall we keep on looking?"

The two disciples found Jesus while He was curing many sick people of their various diseases, healing the lame and the blind and casting out evil spirits. So they asked Him John's question. And this was His reply: "Go back to John and tell him all you have seen and heard here today: how those who were blind can see! The lame are walking without a limp! The lepers are completely healed! The deaf can hear again! The dead come back to life! And the poor are hearing the Good News! And tell him, 'Happy is the one who does not lose his faith in Me.'"

After they left, Jesus talked to the crowd about John. "Who is this man you went out into the Judean wilderness to see?" He asked. "Did you find him weak as grass, moved by every breath of wind? Did you find him dressed in expensive clothes? No! Men who live in luxury are found in palaces, not out in the wilderness! But did you find a prophet? Yes! And more than a prophet! He is the one to whom the Scriptures refer when they say, 'Look! I am sending My messenger ahead of You, to prepare the way before You!' Truly, of all men ever born, none shines more brightly than John the Baptist. And yet, even the lesser lights in the Kingdom of Heaven will be greater than he is!

"And from the time John the Baptist began preaching and baptizing until now, ardent multi-

Matthew 11:3; Luke 7:20-27; Matthew 11:11,12

tudes have been crowding toward the Kingdom of Heaven. For all the Old Testament law and prophets looked forward to the Messiah. Then John appeared, and if you are willing to understand what I mean, he is Elijah, the one the prophets said would come at the time the Kingdom begins. If ever you had willing ears, listen now! The Pharisees and teachers of Moses' Law rejected God's plan for them and refused John's baptism.

"What can I say about such men? With what shall I compare them? These people are like children playing, who say to their little friends, 'We played wedding and you weren't happy, so we played funeral but you weren't sad.' For John the Baptist didn't even drink wine and often went without food, and you say, 'He's crazy.' And I, the Son of Man, feast and drink, and you complain that I am 'a glutton and a drinking man, and hang around with the worst sort of sinners!' But brilliant men like you can justify your every inconsistency!"

Another time one of the Pharisees asked Jesus to come to his home for lunch, and Jesus accepted the invitation. As they sat down to eat, a woman of the streets—a prostitute—who had heard He was there, brought an exquisite flask filled with expensive perfume, and going in, she knelt behind Him at His feet, weeping until His feet were wet with her tears; and she wiped them off with her hair and kissed them and poured the perfume on them.

When Jesus' host, a Pharisee, saw what was

Matt. 11:12-15; Luke 7:30,31; Matt. 11:16-19; Luke 7:36-39

happening and who the woman was, he said to himself, "This proves that Jesus is no prophet, for if God had really sent Him, He would know what kind of woman this one is!"

Then Jesus spoke up and answered his thoughts! "Simon," He said to the Pharisee, "I have something to say to you."

"All right, Teacher," Simon replied, "go ahead."

Then Jesus told him this story: "A man loaned money to two people—$5,000 to one and $500 to the other. But neither of them could pay him back, so he kindly forgave them both, letting them keep the money! Which do you suppose loved him most after that?"

"I suppose the one who owed him the most," answered Simon.

"Correct," Jesus agreed. Then He turned towards the woman and said to Simon, "Look! See this woman kneeling here! When I entered your home, you didn't bother to offer Me water to wash the dust from My feet, but she has washed them with her tears and wiped them with her hair! You refused Me the customary kiss of greeting, but she has kissed My feet again and again from the time I first came in. You neglected the usual courtesy of olive oil to anoint My head, but she has covered My feet with rare perfume. Therefore her sins—and they are many—are forgiven, for she loved Me much; but one who is forgiven little, shows little love!"

Luke 7:39-47

And He said to her, "Your sins are forgiven!"

Then the other men at the table said to themselves, "Who does this man think He is, going around forgiving sins?"

And Jesus said to the woman, "Your faith has saved you; go in peace."

Not long afterward He began a tour of the cities and villages of Galilee to announce the coming of the Kingdom of God, and He took His twelve disciples with Him. Some women from whom He had cast out demons or healed went along too; among them were Mary Magdalene (Jesus had cast seven demons out of her), Joanna, Chuza's wife (Chuza was King Herod's business manager and was in charge of his palace and domestic affairs), Susanna, and many others who were contributing from their private means to the support of Jesus and His disciples.

One day when He returned to the house where He was staying, the crowds began to gather again, and soon the house was so full of visitors that He couldn't even find time to eat! When His friends heard what was happening, they came to try to take Him home with them. "He's out of His mind!" they said.

A demon-possessed man, both blind and dumb, was brought to Jesus, and He healed him, so that he could speak and see. The crowd was amazed. "Can it be that Jesus is the Messiah?" they asked.

But when the Pharisees heard about the miracle,

Luke 7:48-50; Luke 8:1-3; Mark 3:20,21; Matthew 12:22-24

they said, "His trouble is that He's possessed by Satan, king of demons. That's why they obey Him!"

Jesus summoned these men and asked them, using proverbs they all understood, "How can Satan cast out Satan? A kingdom divided against itself will collapse. A home filled with strife and division destroys itself. And if Satan is fighting against himself, how can he accomplish anything? He would never survive! And if, as you claim, I am casting out demons by invoking the powers of Satan, then what power is being used by your own people who are casting them out? Let them answer whether you are being fair! But if I am casting out demons by the Spirit of God, then the Kingdom of God has arrived among you. Satan must be bound before his demons are cast out, just as a strong man must be tied up before his house can be ransacked and his property robbed. Anyone who isn't helping Me is harming Me. Yet even this blasphemy against Me, or any other sin, can be forgiven—except one: Speaking against the Holy Spirit shall never be forgiven, either in this world or in the world to come.

"A tree is identified by its fruit. A tree from a select variety produces good fruit; poor varieties don't. You brood of snakes! How could evil men like you speak what is good and right? For a man's heart determines his speech. A good man's speech reveals the rich treasures within him. An evil-hearted man is filled with venom, and his speech

Mark 3:22-26; Matthew 12:27,28; Mark 3:27; Matthew 12:30-35

reveals it. And I tell you this, that you must give account on judgment day for every idle word you speak. Your words here reflect your fate: either you will be justified by them or you will be condemned."

Matthew 12:35-37

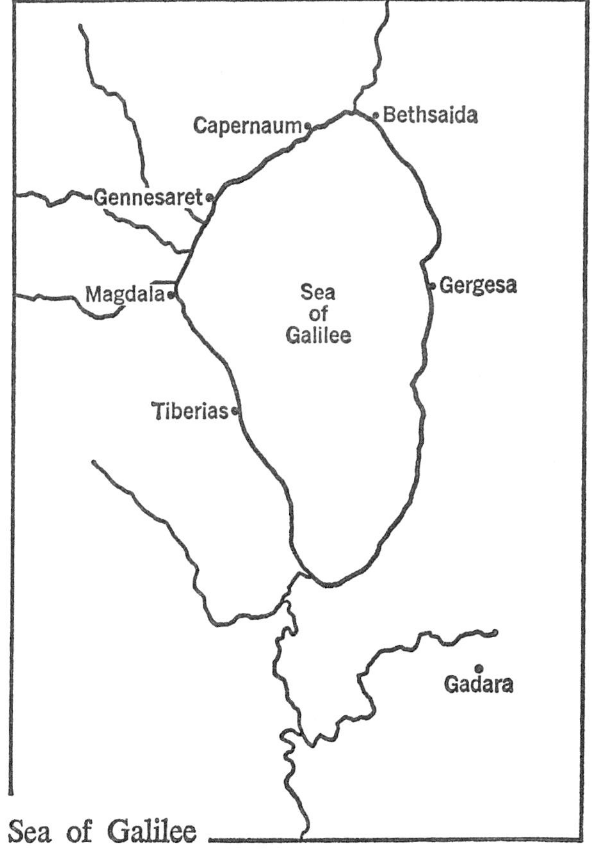

Sea of Galilee

Chapter 14

Hidden Meanings

One day some of the Jewish leaders, including some Pharisees, came to Jesus, asking to see a miracle to prove that He really was the Messiah.

But Jesus replied, "Only an evil, faithless nation would ask for further proof; and none will be given except that of Jonah the prophet! For as Jonah was in the great fish for three days and three nights, so shall I, the Son of Man, be in the heart of the earth three days and three nights.

"The men of Nineveh shall arise against this nation at the judgment, and condemn you. For when Jonah preached to them they repented, and turned to God from all their evil ways. And now a greater than Jonah is here, and you refuse to believe Him. The Queen of Sheba shall rise against this nation in the judgment, and condemn it; for she came from a distant land to hear the wisdom of Solomon; and now a greater than Solomon is here—and you refuse to believe Him.

"This evil nation is like a man possessed by a demon. For if the demon leaves, it goes into the deserts for a while, seeking rest but finding none. Then it says, 'I will return to the man I came from.' So it returns and finds the man's heart clean but empty! Then the demon finds seven other spirits

Matthew 12:38-45

more evil than itself, and all enter the man and live in him. And so that man's last state is far worse than his first!"

Once when His mother and brothers came to see Him, they couldn't even get into the house where He was teaching, because of the crowds. They sent word for Him to come out and talk with them. "Your mother and brothers are outside and want to see You," He was told.

He replied, "Who is My mother? Who are My brothers?" Looking at those around Him He said, "These are My mother and brothers! Anyone who does God's will is My brother, and My sister, and My mother!"

Once again an immense crowd gathered around Him on the beach as He was teaching, so He got into a boat and sat down and talked from there. His usual method of teaching was to tell the people stories. One of them went like this: "A farmer went out to his field to sow grain. As he scattered the seeds on the ground, some of it fell on a footpath and it was trampled on; and the birds came and ate it as it lay exposed. Other seeds fell on shallow soil with rock beneath. These seeds began to grow, but soon withered and died for lack of moisture. Other seeds landed in thistle patches, and the young plants were soon choked out. Still others fell on fertile soil; these grew and produced a crop 100 times as large as he had planted." As He was giving this

Matthew 12:45; Luke 8:19; Mark 3:31-35; Mark 4:1,2; Luke 8:5-8 illustration He said, "If anyone has listening ears, use them now!"

Afterwards, when He was alone His disciples came and asked Him, "Why do you always use these hard-to-understand illustrations?"

He replied, "You are permitted to know some truths about the Kingdom of God that are hidden to those outside the Kingdom. For to him who has will more be given, and he will have great plenty; but from him who has not, even the little he has will be taken away. That is why I use these illustrations, so they will hear and see but not understand.

"This fulfills the prophecy of Isaiah, 'They hear, but don't understand; they look, but don't see! For their hearts are fat and heavy, and their ears are dull, and they have closed their eyes in sleep, so that they won't see and hear and understand and turn to God again that I should heal them.' But blessed are your eyes, for they see; and your ears, for they hear. Truly, many a prophet and godly man longed to see what you have seen, and hear what you have heard, but couldn't.

"Now here is the explanation of the illustration I used about the farmer planting grain: The seed is God's message to men. The farmer I talked about is anyone who brings God's message to others, trying to plant good seed within their lives.

"The hard path where some seed fell represents the heart of a person who hears the good news about the kingdom and doesn't understand it; then

Luke 8:8; Mark 4:10; Matthew 13:10; Mark 4:11; Matthew 13:11-18; Luke 8:11; Mark 4:14; Matthew 13:19

Satan comes and snatches away the seeds from his heart.

"The stony ground represents those who enjoy listening to sermons, but somehow the message never really gets through to them and doesn't take root and grow. They know the message is true, and sort of believe for awhile; but when the hot winds of persecution blow, they lose interest.

"The thorny ground represents the hearts of people who listen to the Good News and receive it, but all too quickly the attractions of this world and the delights of wealth, and the search for success and lure of nice things come in and crowd out God's message from their hearts, so that no crop is produced.

"But the good soil represents honest, good-hearted people. They listen to God's words and cling to them and steadily spread them to others who also soon believe. They produce a plentiful harvest for God—30, 60, or even 100 times as much as was planted in their hearts."

Then He asked them, "When someone lights a lamp, does he put a box over it to shut out the light? Of course not! The light couldn't be seen or used. A lamp is placed on a stand to shine and be useful! All that is now hidden will someday come to light. If you have ears, listen! But be sure to put into practice what you hear. The more you do this, the more you will understand what I tell you.

Matthew 13:19; Luke 8:13; Mark 4:18,19; Luke 8:15; Mark 4:20-24

"Here is another story illustrating what the Kingdom of God is like: A farmer sowed his field and went away, and as the days went by, the seeds grew and grew without his help! For the soil made the seeds grow. First a leaf-blade pushed through, and later the wheat-heads formed and finally the grain ripened, and then the farmer came at once with his sickle and harvested it."

Here is another illustration Jesus used: "The Kingdom of Heaven is like a farmer sowing good seed in his field; but one night as he slept, his enemy came and sowed thistles among the wheat. When the crop began to grow, the thistles grew too. The farmer's men came and told him, 'Sir, the field where you planted that choice seed is full of thistles!'

" 'An enemy has done it,' he said.

" 'Shall we pull the thistles?' they asked.

" 'No,' he replied. 'You'll hurt the wheat if you do. Let both grow together until the harvest, and I will tell the reapers to gather the thistles first and burn them, and put the wheat in the barn.' "

Here is another of His illustrations: "The Kingdom of Heaven is like a tiny mustard seed planted in a field. It is the smallest of all seeds, but becomes the largest of plants and grows into a tree where birds can come and find shelter."

He also used this example: "The Kingdom of Heaven can be compared to a woman making bread! She takes a measure of flour and mixes in

Mark 4:26-29; Matthew 13:24-33

the yeast until it permeates every part of the dough."

Jesus constantly used these illustrations when speaking to the crowds. In fact, because the prophets said that He would use so many, He never spoke to them without at least one illustration. For it had been prophesied, "I will talk in parables; I will explain mysteries hidden since the beginning of time."

Then He went into the house, leaving the crowds outside. His disciples asked Him to explain to them the illustration of the thistles and the wheat.

"All right," He said, "I am the farmer who sows the choice seed. The field is the world, and the choice seed represents the people of the Kingdom; the thistles are the people belonging to Satan. The enemy who sowed the thistles among the wheat is the devil; the harvest is the end of the world, and the reapers are the angels.

"Just as in this story the thistles are separated and burned, so shall it be at the end of the world: I will send My angels and they will separate out of the Kingdom every temptation and all who are evil, and throw them into the furnace and burn them. There shall be weeping and gnashing of teeth. Then the godly shall shine as the sun in their Father's Kingdom. Let those with ears, listen!

"The Kingdom of Heaven is like a treasure discovered in a field. In his excitement, the man who

Matthew 13:33-44

discovers it sells everything he owns to get enough money to buy the field.

"Again the Kingdom of Heaven is like a pearl merchant on the lookout for choice pearls. He discovered a real find—a pearl of great value—and sold all he had to purchase it!

"Again, the Kingdom of Heaven can be illustrated by a fisherman—he casts a net into the water and gathers in fish of every kind, valuable and worthless. When the net is full, he drags it up onto the beach and sits down and sorts out the edible ones into crates and throws the others away. That is the way it will be at the end of the world—the angels will come and separate the wicked people from the godly, casting the wicked into the fire; there shall be weeping and gnashing of teeth. Do you understand?"

"Yes," they said, "we do."

Then He added, "Those experts in Jewish law who are now My disciples have double treasures—from the Old Testament as well as the New!"

When Jesus had finished these illustrations, He returned to His home town, Nazareth in Galilee, and taught there in the synagogue and astonished everyone with His wisdom and His miracles!

Matthew 13:44-54

Chapter 15

Power Unlimited

Midsummer, A.D. 28

At the Sea of Galilee one day Jesus noticed how large the crowd was getting, and He told His disciples to go across to the other side of the lake. Just then one of the Jewish religious teachers said to Him, "Teacher, I will follow You no matter where You go!"

But Jesus said, "Foxes have dens and birds have nests, but I, the Son of Man, have no home of My own—no place for My head."

Another of His followers said, "Sir, let me first go and bury my father."

But Jesus told him, "Follow Me now! Let those who are spiritually dead care for their own dead."

Then He got into a boat and started across the lake with His disciples. Soon a terrible storm arose. High waves began to break into the boat until it was nearly full of water and about to sink.

Jesus was asleep at the back of the boat with His head on a cushion. Frantically they wakened Him, shouting, "Lord, save us! We're sinking! Don't You even care that we are all about to drown?"

Jesus answered, "O you men of little faith! Why are you so frightened?" Then He stood up and

Matthew 8:18-23; Mark 4:37,38; Matthew 8:25,26

rebuked the wind and said to the sea, "Quiet down!" And the wind fell, and there was a great calm!

And He asked them, "Why were you so fearful? Don't you even yet have confidence in Me?"

And they were filled with awe and said among themselves, "Who is this man, that even the winds and seas obey Him?"

So they arrived at the other side, in the Gerasene country across the lake from Galilee. As He was climbing out of the boat, a man from the city of Gadara came to meet Him. This man had been demon-possessed for a long time. Homeless and naked, he lived in a cemetery among the tombs. He had such strength that whenever he was put into handcuffs and shackles—as he often was—he snapped the handcuffs from his wrists and smashed the shackles and walked away. No one was strong enough to control him. All day long and through the night he would wander among the tombs and in the wild hills, screaming and cutting himself with sharp pieces of stone.

When Jesus was still far out on the water, the man had seen Him and had run to meet Him, and fell down before Him. Then Jesus spoke to the demon within the man and said, "Come out, you evil spirit."

It gave a terrible scream, shrieking, "What are You going to do to me, Jesus, Son of the Most High God? For God's sake, don't torture me!"

Mark 4:39-41; Luke 8:26,27; Mark 5:3-8

"What is your name?" Jesus asked, and the demon replied, "Legion, for there are many of us here within this man."

They kept begging Him not to order them into the Bottomless Pit.

Now, as it happened, there was a huge herd of hogs rooting around on the hill above the lake. "Send us into those hogs," the demons begged, and Jesus gave them permission. Then the evil spirits came out of the man and entered the hogs, and the entire herd plunged down the steep hillside into the lake and was drowned.

The herdsmen fled to the nearby towns and countryside, spreading the news as they ran. Everyone rushed out to see for themselves, and a large crowd soon gathered where Jesus was; but as they saw the man sitting there, fully clothed and perfectly sane, they were frightened. Those who saw what happened were telling everyone about it, and the crowd began pleading with Jesus to go away and leave them alone! So He got back into the boat.

The man who had been possessed by the demons begged Jesus to let him go along. But Jesus said no. "Go home to your friends," He told him, "and tell them what wonderful things God has done for you; and how merciful He has been." So the man started off to visit the Ten Towns of that region and began to tell everyone about the great things Jesus had done for him; and they were awestruck by his story.

When Jesus had gone across by boat to the other

Mark 5:9; Luke 8:31; Mark 5:11-21

side of the lake, the crowds received Him with open arms, for they had been waiting for Him.

And now a man named Jairus, a leader of a Jewish synagogue, came and fell down at Jesus' feet, pleading with Him to heal his only child, a little girl twelve years old. "She is at the point of death," he said in desperation. "Please come and place Your hands on her and make her live." Jesus went with him, pushing through the crowds.

Among the crowd was a woman who had been sick for twelve years with a hemorrhage. She had suffered much from many doctors through the years and had become poor from paying them, and was no better but, in fact, was worse. She had heard all about the wonderful miracles Jesus did, and that is why she came up behind Him through the crowd and touched His clothes. For she thought to herself, "If I can just touch His clothing, I will be healed."

And sure enough, as soon as she had touched Him, the bleeding stopped and she knew she was well! Jesus realized at once that healing power had gone out from Him, so He turned around in the crowd, "Who touched Me?" Jesus asked.

Everyone denied it, and Peter said, "Master, so many are crowding against You . . ."

But Jesus said, "No, it was someone who deliberately touched Me, for I felt healing power go out from Me."

When the woman realized that Jesus knew, she began to tremble and fell down before Him and

Mark 5:21; Luke 8:40,41; Mark 5:23; Luke 8:42;
Mark 5:25-30; Luke 8:45-47

told why she had touched Him and that she was now well. He said to her, "Daughter, your faith has healed you! Go in peace."

While He was still talking with her, a messenger arrived from the Jairus home with the news that his little girl was dead. "She's gone," they told her father; "there is no use troubling the Teacher now."

But Jesus ignored their comments and said to Jairus, "Don't be afraid. Just trust Me." Then Jesus halted the crowd and wouldn't let anyone go on with Him to Jairus' home except Peter and James and John. The home was filled with mourning people, but He said, "Stop the weeping! She isn't dead; she is only asleep!" This brought scoffing and laughter, for they all knew she was dead. He took her by the hand and called, "Get up, little girl!" And at that moment her life returned and she jumped up! And He told them to give her something to eat! Her parents were overcome with happiness, but Jesus insisted that they not tell anyone the details of what had happened.

As Jesus was leaving her home, two blind men followed Him, shouting, "O Son of King David, have mercy on us."

They followed Him into the house where He was staying, and Jesus asked them, "Do you believe I can make you see?"

"Yes, Lord," they told Him, "we do."

Then He touched their eyes and said, "Because of your faith, the miracle will happen!" And sud-

Luke 8:47-49; Mark 5:36,37; Luke 8:52-56; Matthew 9:27-30

denly, they could see! Jesus sternly warned them not to tell anyone about it, but instead they spread His fame all over town.

Going on from there, Jesus met a man who couldn't speak because he was possessed by a demon. Jesus cast out the demon, and immediately the man began to talk! The crowds marveled. "We've never seen anything like this before," they said. But the Pharisees said, "He can cast out demons because he is demon-possessed himself—possessed by Satan, the demon king!"

Autumn, A.D. 28

Soon afterwards He left that section of the country and returned with His disciples to Nazareth, His home town. The next Sabbath He went to the synagogue to teach, and the people were astonished at His wisdom and His miracles, because He was just a local man like themselves. "He's no better than we are," they said. "He's just a carpenter, Mary's boy, and a brother of James and Joseph, Judas and Simon. And His sisters live right here among us." And they were offended!

Then Jesus told them, "A prophet is honored everywhere except in his home town and among his relatives and by his own family!" And because of their unbelief He couldn't do any mighty miracles among them, except to heal a few sick people by placing His hands on them! And He could hardly

Matthew 9:30-34; Mark 6:1-6

accept the fact that they wouldn't believe in Him. Then He went out among the villages, teaching.

Jesus went into all the cities and villages, teaching in the Jewish synagogues, announcing the good news about the Kingdom, and healing people of every kind of illness. He was filled with pity for the crowds that came, because their problems were so great and they didn't know what to do or where to go for help, like sheep without a shepherd.

Then He said to His disciples, "The harvest is so great, and the workers are so few. Pray therefore to the One Who is in charge of the harvesting, and ask Him to send out more workers into His harvest fields."

Mark 6:6; Matthew 9:35-38

Chapter 16

On Their Own

Jesus called His twelve disciples to Him, and gave them authority over evil spirits, to cast them out, and over all sickness and diseases. Jesus sent them out two by two with these instructions: "Don't minister to the Gentiles, or the Samaritans, but to the lost sheep of Israel. And as you go, preach that the Kingdom of Heaven is near. Heal the sick, raise the dead, cure the lepers, and cast out demons. Give as freely as you have received!

"Don't take any money with you, or any duffle bag with extra clothes and shoes, or even a walking stick, for those you help should feed and care for you. Whenever you enter a city or village, search for a godly man, and stay in his home. Stay at one home in each village—don't shift around from house to house while you are there. When you stop at a house, be friendly, and if it is a godly home, give it your blessing; if not, keep the blessing. If you are not welcomed in a city, or a home, and those living there won't listen to you, shake off the dust of that place from your feet as you leave them. Truly, the wicked cities of Sodom and Gomorrah will be better off at judgment day than they.

"I am sending you out as sheep among wolves. Be as wary as serpents and harmless as doves. But

Matthew 10:1; Mark 6:7; Matthew 10:5-11; Mark 6:10; Matthew 10:12-16 beware! For you will be arrested and tried, and whipped in the synagogues. Yes, and you must stand trial before governors and kings for My sake, giving you an opportunity to tell them about Me, and to testify to the world. When you are arrested, don't worry about what to say at your trial, for you will be given the right words at the right time. It won't be you doing the talking—it will be the Spirit of your heavenly Father speaking through you!

"Brother shall betray brother to death, and fathers shall betray their own children! And children shall rise against parents, and cause their death. Everyone shall hate you because you belong to Me. But all of you who endure to the end shall be saved.

"When you are persecuted in one city, flee to the next! For I will return before you have fled through them all! A student is not greater than his teacher, nor a servant above his master. The student shares his teacher's fate, and the servant his master's! And since I, the master of the household, have been called 'Satan,' how much more will you! But don't be afraid of those who threaten you. For the time is coming when the truth will be revealed: Their secret plots will become public information. What I tell you now in the gloom, shout abroad when daybreak comes. What I whisper in your ears, proclaim from the housetops!

"Don't be afraid of those who can only kill the body—but can't touch your soul! Fear only God

Matthew 10:17-28

who can destroy both soul and body in hell. Not one sparrow (What do they cost? Two for a penny?) can fall to the ground without your Father knowing it! And the very hairs of your head are all numbered! So don't worry! You are more valuable to Him than many sparrows!

"If anyone publicly acknowledges Me, I will acknowledge him in front of My Father in heaven. But if anyone publicly denies Me, I will deny him in front of My Father in heaven.

"Don't imagine that I came to bring peace to the earth! No, rather, a sword! I have come to set a man against his father, and a daughter against her mother, and a daughter-in-law against her mother-in-law—a man's opponents will be within his own home!

"But if you love your father and mother more than you love Me, you are not worthy of being Mine. And if you love your son or daughter more than Me, you are not worthy of being Mine. And if you will not take up your cross and follow Me, you are not worthy of being Mine. If you cling to your life, you will lose it, but if you give it up for Me, you will save it!

"Those who welcome you are welcoming Me! And when they welcome Me they are welcoming God, who sent Me. If you welcome a prophet because he is a man of God, you will be given the same reward a prophet gets. And if you welcome good and godly men because of their godliness, you

Matthew 10:28-41

will be given a reward like theirs! And if, as My representatives, you give even a cup of cold water to a little child, you will surely be rewarded."

So the disciples went out, telling everyone they met to turn from sin. And they cast out many demons, and healed many sick people by anointing them with olive oil.

When Jesus had finished giving His instructions to His twelve disciples, He went off preaching in the cities where they were scheduled to be.

Early A.D. 29

King Herod soon heard about Jesus, for His miracles were talked about everywhere. The king thought Jesus was John the Baptist come back to life again. And the people were saying, "No wonder He can do such miracles." Others thought Jesus was Elijah the ancient prophet, now returned to life again; still others claimed He was a new prophet like the great ones of the past. "No," Herod said, "it is John, the man I beheaded. He has come back from the dead." And he tried to see Him.

Herod had sent soldiers to arrest and imprison John because he kept saying it was wrong for the king to marry Herodias, his brother Philip's wife. Herodias wanted John killed in revenge, but without Herod's approval she was powerless. And Herod respected John, knowing that he was a good and holy man, and so he kept him under his protec-

Matthew 10:41,42; Mark 6:12,13; Matthew 11:1; Mark 6:14-16; Luke 9:9; Mark 6:17-20

tion. And Herod was disturbed whenever he talked with John, but even so he liked to listen to him.

Herodias' chance finally came. It was Herod's birthday and he gave a stag party for his palace aides, army officers, and the leading citizens of Galilee. Then Herodias' daughter came in and danced before them and greatly pleased them all. "Ask me for anything you like," the king vowed, "even half of my kingdom, and I will give it to you!"

She went out and consulted her mother, who told her, "Ask for John the Baptist's head!" So she hurried back to the king and announced, "I want the head of John the Baptist—right now—on a tray!"

Then the king was sorry, but he was embarrassed to break his oath in front of his guests. So he sent one of his bodyguards to the prison to cut off John's head and bring it to them. The soldier killed John in the prison and brought back his head on a tray, and gave it to the girl and she took it to her mother. When John's disciples heard what had happened, they came for his body and buried it in a tomb.

As soon as Jesus heard what had happened, He went off by Himself in a boat to a remote area. But the crowds saw where He was headed, and followed by land from many villages.

The apostles returned to Jesus from their tour and told Him all they had done and what they had said to the people they visited.

Mark 6:20-29; Matthew 14:13; Mark 6:30

Then Jesus told them, "Let's get away from the crowds for awhile and rest." For so many people were coming and going that they scarcely had time to eat! And they left by boat for a quieter spot. But many people saw them leaving and recognized them and ran on ahead along the shore and met them as they landed! So the usual vast crowd was there as He stepped from the boat; and He had pity on them because they were like sheep without a shepherd. And He taught them many things they needed to know.

Mark 6:31-34

Chapter 17

Something for Nothing

Near April, A.D. 29

And a huge crowd, many of them pilgrims on their way to Jerusalem for the annual Passover celebration, were following Him wherever He went, to watch Him heal the sick. So when Jesus went up into the hills and sat down with His disciples around Him, He soon saw a great multitude of people climbing the hill, looking for Him. Turning to Philip He asked, "Philip, where can we buy bread to feed all these people?" He was testing Philip, for He already knew what He was going to do!

Philip replied, "It would take a fortune to begin to do it!"

Then Andrew, Simon Peter's brother, spoke up. "There's a youngster here with five barley loaves and a couple of fish! But what good is that with all this mob?"

"Tell everyone to sit down," Jesus ordered. And all 5,000 of them (that was the approximate count of the men only) sat down on the grassy slopes in groups of 50 or 100. Then Jesus took the loaves and gave thanks to God and passed them out to the people. Afterwards He did the same with the fish.

John 6:2-10; Mark 6:40; John 6:11

And everyone had all he wanted. "Now gather the scraps," Jesus told His disciples, "so that nothing is wasted." And 12 baskets were filled with the left-overs!

When the people realized what a great miracle had happened, they exclaimed, "Surely, He is the Prophet we have been expecting!" Jesus saw that they were ready to take Him by force and make Him their king, so He went higher into the mountains alone. That evening His disciples went down to the shore to wait for Him. But as darkness fell and Jesus still hadn't come back, they got into the boat and headed across the lake toward Capernaum. But soon a gale swept down upon them as they rowed, and the sea grew very rough.

About four o'clock in the morning when they were three or four miles out Jesus came to them, walking on the water! The disciples screamed in terror when they saw Him, for they thought He was a ghost. But Jesus immediately spoke to them and reassured them, telling them not to be afraid!

Then Peter said, "Sir, if it is really You, tell me to come over to You, walking on the water!"

"Yes," the Lord said, "Come!" So Peter went over the side of the boat and walked on the water towards Jesus!

But when Peter looked around at the high waves, he was terrified and began to sink! "Save me, Lord!" he shouted.

Instantly Jesus reached out His hand and rescued

John 6:11-18; Matthew 14:25-31

him. "O man of little faith," Jesus said, "why did you doubt?" And when they had climbed into the boat, the wind stopped.

The others sat there, awestruck. "You really are the Son of God," they said.

When they arrived at Gennesaret, on the other side of the lake, they moored the boat, and climbed out. The people standing around recognized Him at once, and ran throughout the whole area to spread the news of His arrival, and began carrying sick folks to Him on mats and stretchers. Wherever He went—in villages and cities, and out on the farms—they laid the sick in the market plazas, and streets and begged Him to let them at least touch the fringes of His clothes; and as many as touched Him were healed.

The next morning, back across the lake, crowds began gathering on the shore, waiting to see Jesus. For they knew that He and His disciples had come over together and that the disciples had gone off in their boat, leaving Him behind. Several small boats from Tiberias were nearby, so when the people saw that Jesus wasn't there, or His disciples, they got into the boats and went across to Capernaum to look for Him. When they arrived and found Him, they said, "Sir, how did You get here?"

Jesus replied, "The truth of the matter is that you want to be with Me because I fed you, not because you believe in Me. But you shouldn't be so concerned about perishable things like food. No, spend

Matthew 14:31-33; Mark 6:53-56; John 6:22-27

your energy seeking the eternal life that I, the Son of Man, can give you. For God the Father has sent Me for this very purpose."

They replied, "What should we do to satisfy God?"

Jesus told them, "This is the will of God, that you believe in the one He has sent."

They replied, "You must show us more miracles if You want us to believe You are the Messiah. Give us free bread every day, like our fathers had while they journeyed through the wilderness! As the Scriptures say, 'Moses gave them bread from Heaven.' "

Jesus said, "Moses didn't give it to them! My Father did. And now He offers you true Bread from heaven. The true Bread is a Person—the one sent by God from heaven, and He gives life to the world."

"Sir," they said, "give us that bread every day of our lives!"

Jesus replied, "I am the Bread of Life! No one coming to Me will ever be hungry again! Those believing in Me will never thirst! But the trouble is, as I have told you before, you haven't believed even though you have seen Me. But some will come to Me—those the Father has given Me—and I will never, never reject them. For I have come here from heaven to do the will of God who sent Me, not to have My own way! And this is the will of God, that I should not lose even one of all those

John 6:27-39

He has given Me, but that I should raise them to eternal life at the Last Day! For it is My Father's will that everyone who sees His Son and believes on Him should have eternal life, and that I should raise him at the Last Day."

Then the Jews began to murmur against Him because He claimed to be the Bread from heaven. "What?" they exclaimed. "Why, He is merely Jesus, the son of Joseph, whose father and mother we know. What is this He is saying, that He came down from heaven?"

But Jesus replied, "Don't murmur among yourselves about My saying that! For no one can come to Me unless the Father who sent Me draws him to Me, and at the Last Day I will bring them all back to life. As it is written in the Scriptures, 'They shall all be taught of God.' Those the Father speaks to, who learn the truth from Him, will be attracted to Me. Not that anyone actually sees the Father, for only I have seen Him. How earnestly I tell you this—anyone who believes in Me already has eternal life!

"Yes, I am the Bread of Life! There was no real life in that bread from the skies, which was given to your fathers in the wilderness, for they all died. But there is such a thing as Bread from heaven giving eternal life to everyone who eats it! And I am that Living Bread that came down out of heaven. Anyone eating this Bread shall live forever; this Bread is My flesh, given to redeem humanity."

John 6:39-52

Then the Jews began arguing with each other about what He meant. "How can this man give us His flesh to eat?" they asked.

So Jesus said it again, "With all the earnestness I possess I tell you this: Unless you eat the flesh of the Son of Man and drink His blood, you cannot have eternal life within you. But anyone who eats My flesh and drinks My blood has eternal life, and I will raise him at the Last Day. For My flesh is the true food, and My blood is the true drink. Everyone who eats My flesh and drinks My blood is in Me, and I in him.

"I live by the power of the living Father who sent Me, and in the same way, those who partake of Me shall live because of Me! I am the true Bread from heaven; and anyone who eats this Bread shall live forever, and not die as your fathers did—though they ate bread from heaven."

He preached the above sermon in the synagogue in Capernaum.

Even His disciples said, "This is very hard to understand. Who can tell what He means?"

Jesus knew within Himself that His disciples were complaining and said to them, "Does this offend you? Then what will you think if you see Me, the Son of Man, return to heaven again?

"Only the Holy Spirit gives eternal life. Those born only once (the physical birth) will never receive this gift. But now I have told you how to get this true spiritual life. But some of you don't be-

John 6:52-64

lieve Me." For Jesus knew from the beginning who didn't believe and the one who would betray Him. And He remarked, "That is what I meant when I said that no one can come to Me unless the Father attracts him to Me."

At this point many of His disciples turned away and deserted Him. Then Jesus turned to The Twelve and asked, "Are you going too?"

Simon Peter replied, "Master, to whom shall we go? You alone have the words that give eternal life, and we believe them and know You are the holy Son of God."

Then Jesus said, "I chose the twelve of you, and one is a devil." He was speaking of Judas, son of Simon Iscariot, one of The Twelve, who would betray Him.

John 6:65-71

Chapter 18

Washing vs. Cleanliness

One day some Jewish religious leaders arrived from Jerusalem to investigate Him and noticed that some of His disciples failed to follow the usual Jewish rituals before eating. For the Jews, especially the Pharisees, will never eat until they have sprinkled their arms to the elbows, as required by their ancient traditions. So when they come home from the market, they must always sprinkle themselves with water before touching any food. There are other examples of some of the laws and regulations they have had for centuries, and still have, such as their ceremony of cleansing for pots, pans and dishes.

So the religious leaders asked Him, "Why don't Your disciples follow our age-old customs? For they eat without first performing the washing ceremony."

Jesus replied, "You bunch of hypocrites! Isaiah the prophet described you very well when he said, 'These people speak very prettily about the Lord, but they have no love for Him at all. Their worship is a farce, for they claim that God commands the people to obey their petty rules.' How right Isaiah was! For you ignore God's specific orders and substitute your own traditions!

Mark 7:1-8

"You are beautifully rejecting God's laws and trampling them under your feet for the sake of your traditions. For instance, Moses gave you this law from God: 'Honor your father and mother.' And he said that anyone who speaks against his father or mother must die. But you say it is perfectly all right for a man to disregard his needy parents, telling them, 'Sorry, I can't help you! for I have given to God what I could have given to you!' And so you break the law of God in order to protect your man-made tradition. And this is only one example. There are many, many others."

Then Jesus called again to the crowd to come and hear. "All of you listen," He said, "and try to understand. Your souls aren't harmed by what you eat, but by what you think and say!"

Then He went into a house to get away from the crowds, and His disciples came and told Him, "You offended the Pharisees by what You just said!"

Jesus replied, "Every plant not planted by My Father shall be rooted up, so ignore them. They are blind guides guiding the blind, and both will fall into a ditch."

Then Peter asked Jesus to explain what He meant when He said that people are not defiled by non-kosher food.

"Don't you understand?" Jesus asked him. "Don't you see that anything you eat simply passes through the digestive tract and out again?" By saying this He showed that every kind of food is

Mark 7:9-17; Matthew 15:10-17

kosher. And then He added, "It is the thought life that pollutes. For from within, out of men's hearts, come evil thoughts of lust, theft, murder, adultery, wanting what belongs to others, wickedness, deceit, lewdness, envy, slander, pride, and all other folly. These are what defile; but there is no spiritual defilement from eating without going through the ritual of ceremonial handwashing!"

He left Galilee and went to the region of Tyre and Sidon, and tried to keep it a secret that He was there, but couldn't. For as usual the news of His arrival spread fast. Right away a woman came to Him whose little girl was possessed by a demon. She had heard about Jesus and now she came and fell at His feet pleading, "Have mercy on me, O Lord, King David's son! For my daughter has a demon within her, and it torments her constantly." But she was Syrophoenician—a "despised Gentile!"

Jesus gave her no reply—not even a word!

Then His disciples urged Him to send her away. "Tell her to get going," they said, "for she is bothering us with all her begging."

Then He said to the woman, "I was sent to help the Jews, not the Gentiles!"

But she came and worshiped Him and pled again, "Sir, help me!"

Jesus told her, "First I should help My own family—the Jews! It isn't right to take the children's food and throw it to the dogs!"

She replied, "That's true, Sir, but even the pup-

Mark 7:19-22; Matthew 15:20; Mark 7:24,25; Matthew 15:22; Mark 7:26; Matthew 15:23-25; Mark 7:27,28

pies under the table are given some scraps from the children's plates!"

"Good!" He said, "You have answered well! Go home in peace, for I have healed your little girl! The demon has left her!" And when she arrived home, her little girl was lying quietly in bed, and the demon was gone.

Early Summer, A.D. 29

Jesus soon returned to the Sea of Galilee, and went up onto a hill and sat down. And a large crowd brought Him their lame, blind, maimed, and those who couldn't speak, and many others, and laid them before Jesus, and He healed them all. What a spectacle it was! Those who hadn't been able to say a word before were talking excitedly, and those with missing arms and legs had new ones; the crippled were walking and jumping around, and those who had been blind were gazing about them! The crowds just marveled, and praised the God of Israel!

A deaf man with a speech impediment was brought to Him, and they begged Jesus to lay His hands on the man and heal him. Jesus led him away from the crowd, and put His fingers into the man's ears, then spat and touched the man's tongue with the spittle. And looking up to heaven He sighed and commanded, "Open!" Instantly the man could hear perfectly and speak plainly!

Mark 7:28-30; Matthew 15:29-31; Mark 7:32-35

Jesus told the crowd not to spread the news, but the more He forbade them, the more they made it known, for they were overcome with utter amazement. Again and again they said, "Everything He does is wonderful; He even corrects deafness and stammering!"

One day about this time as another great crowd gathered, the people ran out of food. Jesus called His disciples and said, "I pity them; for they have been here three days, and have nothing to eat. If I send them home without feeding them, they will faint along on the road! For some of them have come a long distance."

His disciples said, "Are we supposed to find food for them here in the desert?"

"How many loaves of bread do you have?" He asked, and they replied, "Seven."

So He told the crowd to sit down on the ground. Then He took the seven loaves, thanked God, broke them into pieces and passed them to His disciples; and the disciples placed them before the people. They found a few small fish too, which Jesus also blessed and told the disciples to serve. And the whole crowd ate until they were full, and afterwards He sent them home. There were about 4,000 people in the crowd that day and when the scraps were picked up after the meal, there were seven very large basketfuls of them!

Immediately after this He got into a boat with

Mark 7:36,37; Mark 8:1-10

His disciples and came to the region of Dalmanutha.

The Pharisees and Sadducees came and sought to test His claim of being the Messiah. "Do a miracle for us!" they said. "Make something happen in the sky! Then we will believe in You!"

His heart fell when He heard this and He said, "Certainly not! How many more miracles do you people need? You are good at reading the weather signs of the skies—red sky tonight means fair weather tomorrow; red sky in the morning means foul weather all day—but you can't read the obvious signs of the times! This evil, unbelieving nation is asking for some strange sign in the heavens, but no further proof will be given except the kind given to Jonah!" Then Jesus walked out on them! He got back into the boat, and crossed to the other side of the lake.

Now the disciples had forgotten to stock up on food before they left, and had only one loaf of bread in the boat. As they were crossing Jesus said to them very solemnly, "Beware of the yeast of King Herod and of the Pharisees!"

"What does He mean?" the disciples asked each other. They finally decided that He must be talking about their forgetting to bring bread.

Jesus realized what they were discussing and He said, "No, that isn't it at all! Can't you understand? Are your hearts too hard to take it in? As Isaiah said, 'Your eyes are to see with—why don't you

Mark 8:10; Matthew 16:1; Mark 8:11,12; Matthew 16:2,3; Mark 8:13-17

look? Why don't you open your ears and listen?' Don't you remember anything at all? What about the 5,000 men I fed with five loaves of bread? How many basketfuls of scraps did you pick up afterwards?"

"Twelve," they said.

"And when I fed the 4,000 with seven loaves, how much was left?"

"Seven basketfuls," they said.

"How could you even think I was talking about food? But again I say it, 'Beware of the yeast of the Pharisees and Sadducees.' "

Then at last they understood that by "yeast" He meant the wrong teaching of the Pharisees and Sadducees.

Mark 8:18-20; Matthew 16:11,12

Chapter 19

Who Is He, Really?

Midsummer, A.D. 29

Another time when they arrived at Bethsaida, some people brought a blind man to Him and begged Him to touch and heal him. Jesus took the blind man by the hand and led him out of the village, and spit upon his eyes, and laid His hands over them. "Can you see anything now?" Jesus asked him.

The man looked around. "Yes!" he said, "I see men! But I can't see them very clearly; they look like tree trunks walking around!"

Then Jesus placed His hands over the man's eyes again and as he looked intently, his sight was completely restored, and he saw everything clearly, drinking in the sights around him. Jesus sent him home to his family. "Don't even go back to the village first," He said.

When Jesus came to Caesarea Philippi, He asked His disciples, "Who are the people saying I am?"

"Well," they replied, "some say John the Baptist; some, Elijah; some, Jeremiah or one of the other prophets."

Then He asked them, "Who do you think I am?"

Mark 8:22-26; Matthew 16:13-15

Simon Peter answered, "The Christ, the Messiah, the Son of the living God."

"God has blessed you, Simon, son of Jonah," Jesus said, "for My Father in heaven has personally revealed this to you—this is not from any human source. You are Peter, a rock; and upon this rock I will build My church; and all the powers of hell shall not prevail against it. And I will give you the keys of the Kingdom of Heaven; whatever doors you lock on earth shall be locked in heaven; and whatever doors you open on earth shall be open in heaven!"

Then He warned the disciples against telling others that He was the Messiah.

From then on Jesus began to speak plainly to His disciples about going to Jerusalem, and of what would happen to Him there—that He would suffer at the hands of the Jewish leaders, that He would be killed, and that three days later He would be raised to life again. But Peter took Him aside to remonstrate with Him. "Heaven forbid, Lord," he said. "This is not going to happen to You!"

Jesus turned to Peter and said, "Get away from Me, you Satan! You are a dangerous trap to Me. You are thinking merely from a human point of view, and not from God's!"

Then He said to all, "Anyone who wants to follow Me must put aside his own desires and conveniences and carry his cross with him every day and keep close to Me! For anyone who keeps his

Matthew 16:16-23; Luke 9:23; Matthew 16:25

life for himself shall lose it; and anyone who loses his life for Me shall find it again. What profit is there if you gain the whole world—and lose eternal life? What can be compared with the value of eternal life?

"For I, the Son of Man, shall come with My angels in the glory of My Father and judge each person according to his deeds. And anyone who is ashamed of Me and My message in these days of unbelief and sin, I, the Son of Man, will be ashamed of him when I return in the glory of My Father, with the holy angels. Truly, some of you standing here now will live to see Me coming in My Kingdom."

Six days later Jesus took Peter, James and his brother John to the top of a high and lonely hill, and as they watched, His appearance changed so that His face shone like the sun and His clothing became dazzling white. Far more glorious than any earthly process could ever make it! Suddenly Moses and Elijah appeared and were talking with Him! They were splendid in appearance, glorious to see; and they were speaking of His death at Jerusalem, to be carried out in accordance with God's plan.

Peter blurted out, "Lord, it's wonderful that we can be here! If You want me to, I'll make three shelters, one for You and one for Moses and one for Elijah!" He said this just to be talking, for he didn't know what else to say and they were all scared stiff.

But while he was still speaking these words, a

Matthew 16:25-27; Mark 8:38; Matthew 16:28; Matthew 17:1-3; Mark 9:3; Luke 9:31; Matthew 17:4; Mark 9:6,7 cloud covered them, blotting out the sun, and a voice from the cloud said, "This is My beloved Son, and I am wonderfully pleased with Him. Listen to Him. Obey Him."

At this the disciples fell on their faces, terribly frightened. Jesus came over and touched them. "Get up; don't be afraid," He said. And when they looked, only Jesus was with them.

As they were going down the mountain, Jesus commanded them not to tell anyone what they had seen until after He had risen from the dead. So they kept it to themselves, but often talked about it, and wondered what He meant by "rising from the dead."

His disciples asked, "Why do the Jewish leaders insist Elijah must return before the Messiah comes?"

Jesus replied, "They are right. Elijah must come and set everything in order. And, in fact, he has already come, but he wasn't recognized, and was badly mistreated just as the prophets had predicted. And I, the Son of Man, shall also suffer at their hands."

Then the disciples realized He was speaking of John the Baptist.

At the bottom of the mountain, they found a great crowd surrounding the other nine disciples, as some Jewish leaders argued with them. The crowd watched Jesus in awe as He came towards them,

Mark 9:7; Matthew 17:5-9; Mark 9:10; Matthew 17:10-12; Mark 9:12; Matthew 17:13; Mark 9:14,15 and then ran to greet Him. "What's all the argument about?" He asked.

One of the men in the crowd spoke up and said, "Teacher, I brought my son for You to heal—he can't talk because he is possessed by a demon. And whenever the demon is in control of him it dashes him to the ground and makes him foam at the mouth and grind his teeth and become rigid. So I begged Your disciples to cast out the demon, but they couldn't do it."

Jesus said to His disciples, "Oh, what tiny faith you have; how much longer must I be with you until you believe? How much longer must I be patient with you? Bring the boy to Me." So they brought the boy, but when he saw Jesus, the demon convulsed the child horribly, and he fell to the ground writhing and foaming at the mouth.

"How long has he been this way?" Jesus asked the father.

And he replied, "Since he was very small. And the demon often makes him fall into the fire or into water to kill him. Oh, have mercy on us and do something if You can."

"If I can?" Jesus asked. "Anything is possible if you have faith."

The father instantly replied, "I do have faith; oh, help me to have more!"

When Jesus saw the crowd was growing, He rebuked the demon. "O demon of deafness and dumbness," He said, "I command you to come out

Mark 9:15-25

of this child and enter him no more!" Then the demon screamed terribly and convulsed the boy again and left him; and the boy lay there limp and motionless, to all appearance dead. A murmur ran through the crowd—"He is dead." But Jesus took him by the hand and helped him to his feet and he stood up and was all right! Awe gripped the people as they saw this display of the power of God.

Afterwards when Jesus was alone with His disciples in the house, they asked Him, "Why couldn't we cast the demon out?"

"Because of your little faith," Jesus told them, "For if you even had faith as small as a tiny mustard seed, you could say to this mountain, 'Move far away,' and it would go. Nothing would be impossible. But this kind of demon won't leave unless you have prayed and gone without food."

Mark 9:25-27; Luke 9:43; Mark 9:28; Matthew 17:20,21

Chapter 20

How to Be Important

Late Summer, A.D. 29

Leaving that region they traveled through Galilee where He tried to avoid all publicity, so that He could spend time with His disciples, teaching them. He would say to them, "I, the Son of Man, am going to be betrayed and killed and three days later I will return to life again." But they didn't understand, and were afraid to ask Him what He meant.

On their arrival in Capernaum, the Temple tax collectors came to Peter and asked him, "Doesn't your Master pay taxes?"

"Sure He does," Peter replied.

Then he went into the house to talk to Jesus about it, but before he had a chance to speak, Jesus asked him, "What do you think, Peter? Do kings levy assessments against their own people, or against conquered foreigners?"

"Against the foreigners," Peter replied.

"Well, then," Jesus said, "the citizens are free! However, we don't want to offend them, so go down to the shore and throw in a line, and open the mouth of the first fish you catch. You will find a coin to cover the taxes for both of us; then go and pay them."

Mark 9:30-32; Matthew 17:24-26

When they were settled in the house where they were to stay, He asked them, "What were you discussing out on the road?" But they were ashamed to answer, for they had been arguing about which of them was the greatest.

He sat down and called them around Him and said, "Anyone wanting to be the greatest must be the least—the servant of all!" Jesus called a small child over to Him and set the little fellow down among them, and said, "Truly, except you turn to God from your sin and become as little children, you will never even get into the Kingdom of Heaven. Therefore anyone who humbles himself as this little child is the greatest in the Kingdom of Heaven. And any of you who welcomes a little child like this because you are Mine is welcoming Me and caring for Me."

One of His disciples, John, told Him one day, "Teacher, we saw a man using Your name to cast out demons; but we told him not to, for he isn't one of our group."

"Don't forbid him!" Jesus said, "For no one doing miracles in My name will quickly turn against Me! For anyone who isn't against us is for us! If anyone so much as gives you a cup of water because you are Christ's—I say this solemnly—he won't lose his reward. But if someone causes one of these little ones who believe in Me to lose his faith—it would be better for that man if a huge millstone were tied around his neck and he were thrown into the sea.

Matthew 17:26; Mark 9:33-35; Matthew 18:2-5; Mark 9:38-42

Woe upon the world for all its evils. Temptation to do wrong is inevitable, but woe to the man who does the tempting.

"If your hand does wrong, cut it off! Better live forever with one hand than be thrown into the unquenchable fires of hell with two! If your foot carries you toward evil, cut it off! Better be lame and live forever than have two feet that carry you to hell. And if your eye is sinful, gouge it out! Better enter the Kingdom of God half blind than to have two eyes and see the fires of hell, where the worm never dies, and the fire never goes out—where all are salted with fire.

"Good salt is worthless if it loses its saltiness; it can season nothing. So don't you lose your flavor! Live in peace with each other instead of arguing like that.

"Beware that you don't look down upon a single one of these little children. For, I tell you, in heaven their angels have constant access to My Father.

"And I, the Son of Man, came to save the lost. If a man has a hundred sheep, and one wanders away and is lost, what will he do? Won't he leave the ninety-nine others and go into the hills to search for the lost? And if he finds it, he will rejoice over it more than over the ninety-nine others safe at home! Just so, it is not My Father's will that even one of these little ones should perish.

Mark 9:42; Matthew 18:7; Mark 9:43-50; Matthew 18:10-13

"If a brother sins against you, go to him privately and confront him with his fault. If he listens and confesses it, you have won back a brother. But if not, then take one or two others with you and go back to him again, proving everything you say by these witnesses. If he still refuses to listen, then take your case to the church, and if the church's verdict favors you, but he won't accept it, then the church should excommunicate him. And I tell you this—whatever you bind on earth is bound in heaven, and whatever you free on earth will be freed in heaven.

"I also tell you this—if two of you agree down here on earth concerning anything you ask for, My Father in heaven will do it for you. For where two or three gather together because they are Mine, I will be right there among them."

Then Peter came to Him and asked, "Sir, how often should I forgive a brother who sins against me? Seven times?"

"No!" Jesus replied, "seventy times seven! The Kingdom of Heaven can be compared to a king who decided to bring his accounts up to date. In the process, one of his debtors was brought in who owed him $10,000,000! He couldn't pay, so the king ordered him sold for the debt, also his wife and children and everything he had.

"But the man fell down before the king, his face in the dust, and said, 'Oh, sir, be patient with me and I will repay it all.' Then the king was filled with pity for him and released him and forgave his debt!

"But when the man left the king, he went to a man who owed him $2,000 and grabbed him by the throat and demanded instant payment. The man fell down before him and begged him to give him a little time. 'Be patient and I will pay it,' he pled. But his creditor wouldn't wait. He had the man arrested and jailed until the debt would be paid in full.

"Then the man's friends went to the king and told him what had happened. And the king called before him the man he had forgiven and said, 'You evil-hearted wretch! Here I forgave you all that tremendous debt you owed me, just because you asked me to—shouldn't you have mercy on others, just as I had mercy on you?' Then the angry king sent the man to the torture chamber until he had paid every last penny due. So shall My heavenly Father do to you if you refuse to truly forgive your brothers."

Matthew 18:26-35

So the crowd was divided about him.

PART 3

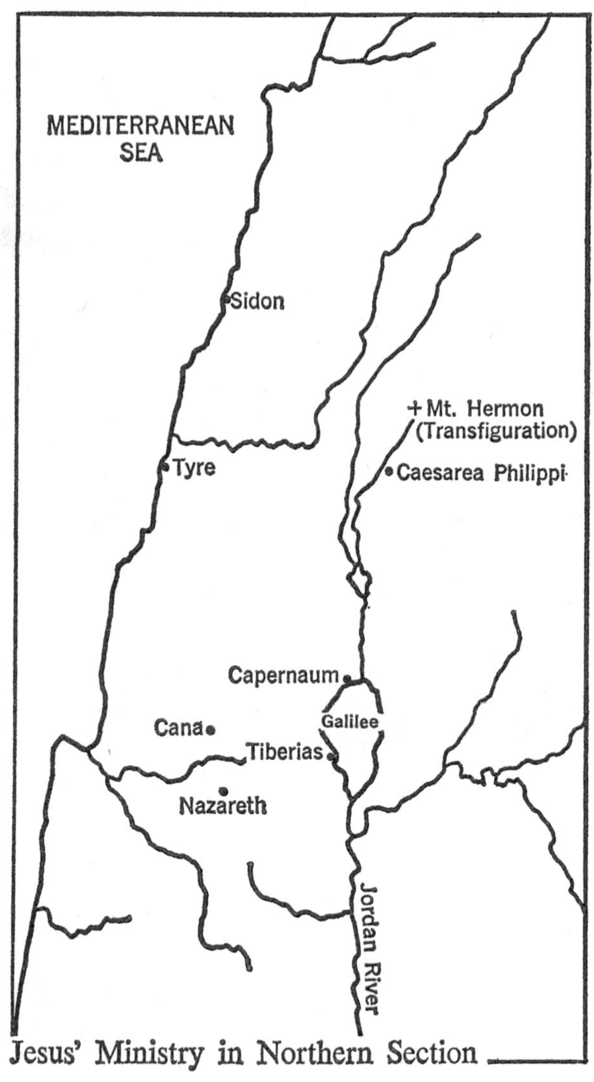

Jesus' Ministry in Northern Section

Chapter 21

Contrary Opinions

October, A.D. 29

As the time drew near for His return to heaven, He moved steadily onward towards Jerusalem with an iron will.

Soon it was time for the Tabernacle Ceremonies, one of the annual Jewish holidays, and Jesus' brothers urged Him to go to Judea for the celebration. "Go where more people can see Your miracles!" they scoffed. "You can't be famous when You hide like this! If You're so great, prove it to the world!" For even His brothers didn't believe in Him.

Jesus replied, "It is not the right time for Me to go now. But you can go anytime and it will make no difference, for the world can't hate you; but it does hate Me, because I accuse it of sin and evil. You go on, and I'll come later when it is the right time." So He remained in Galilee.

But after His brothers had left for the celebration, then He went too, though secretly, staying out of the public eye.

One day He sent messengers ahead to reserve rooms for them in a Samaritan village. But they were turned away! The people of the village re-

Luke 9:51; John 7:2-10; Luke 9:52,53

fused to have anything to do with them because they were headed for Jerusalem! When the word came back of what had happened, James and John said to Jesus, "Master, shall we order fire down from heaven to burn them up?" But Jesus turned and rebuked them and they went on to another village.

As they were walking along, someone said to Jesus, "I will always follow You, no matter where You go."

But Jesus replied, "Remember, I don't even own a place to lay My head. Foxes have dens to live in and birds have nests, but I, the Son of Man, have no earthly home at all."

Another time, when He invited a man to come with Him and be His disciple, the man agreed—but wanted to wait until his father's death.

Jesus replied, "Let those without eternal life concern themselves with things like that. Your duty is to come and preach the coming of the Kingdom of God to all the world."

Another said, "Yes, Lord, I will come, but first let me ask permission of those at home."

But Jesus told him, "Anyone who lets himself be distracted from the work I plan for him is not fit for the Kingdom of God."

The Jewish leaders tried to find Him at the celebration and kept asking if anyone had seen Him. There was a lot of discussion about Him among the crowds. Some said, "He's a wonderful

Luke 9:53-62; John 7:11,12

man," while others said, "No, He is duping the public." But no one had the courage to speak out for Him in public for fear of reprisals from the Jewish leaders.

But midway through the festival, Jesus went up to the Temple and preached openly. The Jewish leaders were surprised when they heard Him. "How can He know so much when He's never been to our schools?" they asked.

So Jesus told them, "I'm not teaching you My own thoughts, but those of God who sent Me. If any of you really determines to do God's will, then you will certainly know whether My teaching is from God or is merely My own. Anyone presenting his own ideas is looking for praise for himself, but anyone seeking to honor the one who sent him is a good and true person. None of you obeys the laws of Moses! So why pick on Me for breaking them? Why kill Me for this?"

The crowd replied, "You're out of Your mind! Who's trying to kill You?"

Jesus replied, "I worked on the Sabbath by healing a man, and you were glad! You work on the Sabbath too—when you obey Moses' law of circumcision (actually, this tradition is older than the Mosaic law), for if the correct time for circumcising your children falls on the Sabbath, you go ahead and do it, as you should. So why should I be condemned for making a man completely well on the

John 7:12-23

Sabbath? Think this through and you will see that I am right."

Some of the people who lived there in Jerusalem and knew what was going on said among themselves, "Isn't this the man they are trying to kill? But here He is, preaching in public, and they say nothing to Him. Can it be that our leaders have learned after all that He really is the Messiah? But how could He be? For we know where this man was born; when Christ comes, He will just appear and no one will know where He comes from."

So Jesus, in a sermon in the Temple, called out, "Yes, you know Me and where I was born and raised, but I am the representative of one you don't know, and He is Truth. I know Him because I was with Him, and He sent Me to you."

Then the Jewish leaders sought to arrest Him; but no hand was laid on Him, for God's time had not yet come. Many among the crowds at the Temple believed on Him. "After all," they said, "what miracles do you expect the Messiah to do that this man hasn't done?"

When the Pharisees heard that the crowds were in this mood, they and the chief priests sent officers to arrest Jesus. But Jesus told them, "Not yet! I am to be here a little longer. Then I shall return to the one who sent Me. You will search for Me but not find Me. And you won't be able to come where I am!"

The Jewish leaders were puzzled by this state-

John 7:23-35

ment. "Where is He planning to go?" they asked. "Maybe He is thinking of leaving the country and going as a missionary among the Jews in other lands or maybe even to the Gentiles! What does He mean about our looking for Him and not being able to find Him, and 'You won't be able to come where I am'?"

On the last day, the climax of the holidays, Jesus shouted to the crowd, "If anyone is thirsty, let him come to Me and drink. For the Scriptures declare that rivers of living water shall flow from the inmost being of anyone who believes in Me." He was speaking of the Holy Spirit, who would be given to everyone believing in Him; but the Spirit had not yet been given, because Jesus had not yet returned to His glory in heaven.

When the crowds heard Him say this, some of them declared, "This man surely is the prophet who will come just before the Messiah." Others said, "He is the Messiah." Still others, "But He can't be! Will the Messiah come from Galilee? For the Scriptures clearly state that the Messiah will be born of the royal line of David, in Bethlehem, the village where David was born." So the crowd was divided about Him. And some wanted Him arrested, but no one touched Him.

The Temple police who had been sent to arrest Him returned to the chief priests and Pharisees. "Why didn't you bring Him in?" they demanded.

John 7:35-45

"He says such wonderful things!" they mumbled. "We've never heard anything like it."

"So you also have been led astray?" the Pharisees mocked. "Is there a single one of us Jewish rulers or Pharisees who believes He is the Messiah? These stupid crowds do, yes; but what do they know about it? A curse upon them anyway!"

Then Nicodemus spoke up. Remember him? He was the Jewish leader who came secretly to interview Jesus. "Is it legal to convict a man before he is even tried?" he asked.

They replied, "Are you a wretched Galilean too? Search the Scriptures and see for yourself—no prophets will come from Galilee!"

The meeting broke up and everybody went home. Jesus returned to the Mount of Olives.

John 7:46-53; John 8:1

Chapter 22

Trapped?

Early the next morning He came again to the Temple. A crowd soon gathered, and He sat down and talked to them.

As He was speaking, the Jewish leaders and Pharisees brought a woman caught in adultery and placed her out in front of the staring crowd. "Teacher," they said to Jesus, "this woman was caught in the very act of adultery. Moses' law says to kill her. What about it?"

They were trying to trap Him into saying something they could use against Him. But Jesus stooped down and wrote in the dust with His finger. They kept demanding an answer, so He stood up again and said, "All right, hurl the stones at her until she dies. But only he who never sinned may throw the first!" Then He stooped down again and wrote some more in the dust.

And the Jewish leaders slipped away one by one, beginning with the eldest, until only Jesus was left in front of the crowd with the woman. Then Jesus stood up again and said to her, "Where are your accusers? Didn't even one of them condemn you?"

"No, Sir," she said.

And Jesus said, "Neither do I. Go and sin no more."

John 8:2-11

Later in one of His talks Jesus said to the people, "I am the Light of the world. So if you follow Me, you won't be stumbling through the darkness, for living light will flood your path."

The Pharisees replied, "You are boasting–and lying!"

Jesus told them, "These claims are true even though I make them concerning Myself. For I know where I came from and where I am going, but you don't know this about Me. You pass judgment on Me without knowing the facts. I am not judging you now; but if I were, it would be an absolutely correct judgment in every respect, for I have with Me the Father who sent Me. Your laws say that if two men agree on something that has happened, their witness is accepted as fact. Well, I am one witness, and My Father who sent Me is the other."

"Where is Your Father?" they asked.

Jesus answered, "You don't know who I am, so you don't know who My Father is. If you knew Me, then you would know Him too."

Jesus made these statements while in the section of the Temple known as the Treasury. But He was not arrested, for His time had not yet run out.

Later He said to them again, "I am going away; and you will search for Me, and die in your sins. And you cannot come where I am going."

The Jews asked, "Is He planning suicide? What does He mean, 'You cannot come where I am going'?"

John 8:12-22

Then He said to them, "You are from below; I am from above. You are of this world; I am not. That is why I said that you will die in your sins; for unless you believe that I am the Messiah, the Son of God, you will die in your sins."

"Tell us who You are," they demanded.

He replied, "I am the one I have always claimed to be. I could condemn you for much and teach you much, but I won't, for I say only what I am told to by the one who sent Me; and He is Truth."

But they still didn't understand that He was talking to them about God. So Jesus said, "When you have killed the Son of Man, then you will realize that I am He and that I have not been telling you My own ideas, but have spoken what the Father taught Me. And He who sent Me is with Me—He has not deserted Me—for I always do those things that are pleasing to Him."

Then many of the Jewish leaders who heard Him say these things began believing Him to be the Messiah. Jesus said to them, "You are truly My disciples if you live as I tell you to, and you will know the truth, and the truth will set you free."

"But we are descendants of Abraham," they said, "and have never been slaves to any man on earth! What do You mean, 'set free'?"

Jesus replied, "You are slaves to sin, every one of you. And slaves don't have rights in their master's home, but the Son has every right there is! So if the Son sets you free, you will indeed be free—even

John 8:23-36

though you are descendants of Abraham! And yet some of you are trying to kill Me because My message does not find a home within your hearts. I am telling you what I saw when I was with My Father. But you are following the advice of your father."

"Our father is Abraham," they declared.

"No!" Jesus replied, "for if he were, you would follow his good example. But instead you are trying to kill Me—and all because I told you the truth I heard from God. Abraham wouldn't do a thing like that! No, you are obeying your real father when you act that way."

They replied, "We were not born out of wedlock —our true Father is God Himself."

Jesus told them, "If that were so, then you would love Me, for I have come to you from God. I am not here on My own, but He sent Me. Why can't you understand what I am saying? It is because you are prevented from doing so! For you are children of your father the Devil, and you love to do the evil things he does. He was a murderer from the beginning and a hater of truth—there is not an iota of truth in him. When he lies, it is perfectly normal; for he is the father of liars. And so when I tell the truth, you just naturally don't believe it!

"Which of you can truthfully accuse Me of one single sin? No one! And since I am telling you the truth, why don't you believe Me? Anyone whose

John 8:37-47

Father is God listens gladly to the words of God. Since you don't, it proves you aren't His children."

"You Samaritan! Foreigner! Devil!" the Jewish leaders snarled. "Didn't we say all along You were possessed by a demon?"

"No," Jesus said, "I have no demon in Me. For I honor My Father—and you dishonor Me. And though I have no wish to make Myself great, God wants this for Me and judges those who reject Me. With all the earnestness I have I tell you this—no one who obeys Me shall ever die!"

The leaders of the Jews said, "Now we know You are possessed by a demon. Even Abraham and the mightiest prophets died, and yet You say that obeying You will keep a man from dying! So You are greater than our father Abraham, who died? And greater than the prophets, who died? Who do You think You are?"

Then Jesus told them this: "If I am merely boasting about Myself, it doesn't count. But it is My Father—and you claim Him as your God—who is saying these glorious things about Me. But you do not even know Him. I do. If I said otherwise, I would be as great a liar as you! But it is true—I know Him and fully obey Him. Your father Abraham rejoiced to see My day. He knew I was coming and was glad."

The Jewish leaders: "You aren't even 50 years old—sure, You've seen Abraham!"

John 8:47-58

Jesus: "The absolute truth is that I was in existence before Abraham was even born!"

At that point the Jewish leaders picked up stones to kill Him. But Jesus was hidden from them, and walked past them and left the Temple.

John 8:58,59

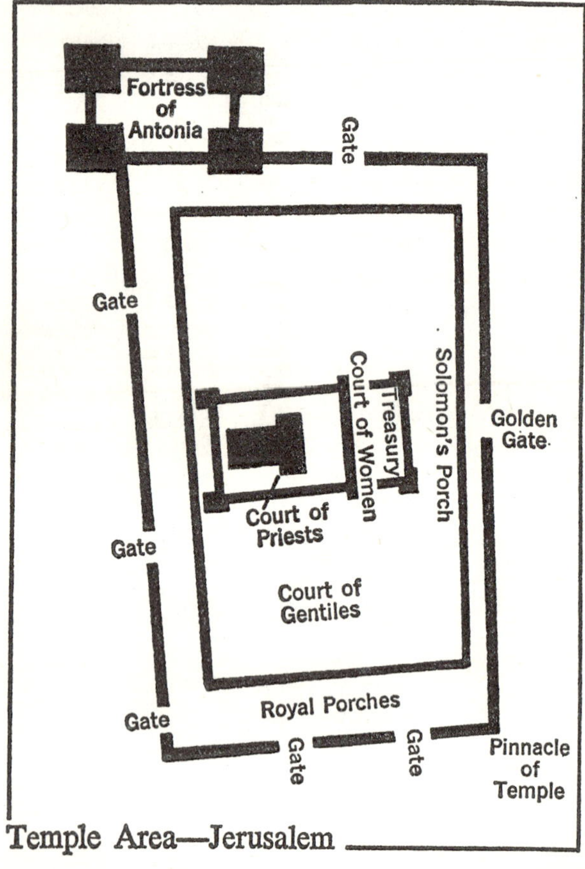

Temple Area—Jerusalem

Chapter 23

To See for the First Time

October—November, A.D. 29

As He was walking along, He saw a man blind from birth.

"Master," His disciples asked Him, "why was this man born blind? Was it a result of his own sins or those of his parents?"

"Neither," Jesus answered. "But to demonstrate the power of God. All of us must quickly carry out the tasks assigned us by the one who sent Me, for there is little time left before the night falls and all work comes to an end. But while I am still here in the world, I give it My light."

Then He spat on the ground and made mud from the spittle and smoothed the mud over the blind man's eyes, and told him, "Go and wash in the Pool of Siloam" (the word "Siloam" means "Sent"). So the man went where he was sent and washed and came back seeing!

His neighbors and others who knew him as a blind beggar asked each other, "Is this the same fellow—that beggar?" Some said yes, and some said no. "It can't be the same man," they thought, "but he surely looks like him!"

And the beggar said, "I am the same man!"

John 9:1-9

Then they asked him how in the world he could see. What had happened? And he told them, "A man they call Jesus made mud and smoothed it over my eyes and told me to go to the Pool of Siloam and wash off the mud. I did, and I can see!"

"Where is He now?" they asked.

"I don't know," he replied.

Then they took the man to the Pharisees. Now as it happened, this all occurred on a Sabbath. Then the Pharisees asked him all about it. So he told them how Jesus had smoothed the mud over his eyes, and when it was washed away, he could see!

Some of them said, "Then this fellow Jesus is not from God, because He is working on the Sabbath!"

Others said, "But how could an ordinary sinner do such miracles?" So there was a deep division of opinion among them.

Then the Pharisees turned on the man who had been blind and demanded, "This man who opened your eyes—who do you say He is?"

"I think He must be a prophet sent from God," the man replied.

The Jewish leaders wouldn't believe he had been blind, until they called in his parents and asked them, "Is this your son? Was he born blind? If so, how can he see?"

His parents replied, "We know this is our son and that he was born blind, but we don't know what happened to make him see, or who did it. He is old enough to speak for himself. Ask him!" They said

John 9:10-22

this in fear of the Jewish leaders who had announced that anyone saying Jesus was the Messiah would be excommunicated.

So for the second time they called in the man who had been blind and told him, "Give the glory to God, not to Jesus, for we know Jesus is an evil person."

"I don't know whether He is good or bad," the man replied, "but I know this: I was blind, and now I see!"

"But what did He do?" they asked. "How did He heal you?"

"Look!" the man exclaimed. "I told you once; didn't you listen? Why do you want to hear it again? Do you want to hear it again? Do you want to become His disciples too?"

Then they cursed him and said, "You are His disciple, but we are disciples of Moses. We know God has spoken to Moses, but as for this fellow, we don't know anything about Him."

"That's very strange!" the man replied. "He can heal blind men, but you don't know anything about Him! Well, God doesn't listen to evil men, but He has open ears to those who worship Him and do His will. Since the world began, there has never been anyone who could open the eyes of someone born blind. If this man were not from God, He couldn't do it."

"You illegitimate bastard, you!" they shouted.

John 9:22-34

"Are you trying to teach us?" And they threw him out.

When Jesus heard what had happened, He found the man and said, "Do you believe in the Messiah?"

The man answered, "Who is He, Sir, for I want to."

"You have seen Him," Jesus said, "and He is speaking to you!"

"Yes, Lord," the man said, "I believe!" And he worshiped Jesus.

Then Jesus told him, "I have come into the world to give sight to those who are spiritually blind and to show those who think they see that they are blind."

The Pharisees who were standing there asked, "Are you saying we are blind?"

"If you were blind, you wouldn't be guilty," Jesus replied. "But your guilt remains because you claim to know what you are doing.

"Anyone refusing to walk through the gate into a sheepfold, who sneaks over the wall, must surely be a thief! For a shepherd comes through the gate! The gatekeeper opens the gate for him, and the sheep hear his voice and come to him; and he calls his own sheep by name and leads them out. He walks ahead of them; and they follow him, for they recognize his voice. They won't follow a stranger, but will run from him, for they don't recognize his voice."

Those who heard Jesus use this illustration didn't

John 9:34-41; John 10:1-6

understand what He meant, so He explained it to them. "I am the Gate for the sheep," He said. "All others who came before Me are thieves and robbers. But the true sheep did not listen to them. Yes, I am the Gate. Those who come in by way of the Gate will be saved and will go in and out and find green pastures. The thief's purpose is to steal, kill and destroy. My purpose is to give eternal life—abundantly!

"I am the Good Shepherd. The Good Shepherd lays down His life for the sheep. A hired man will run when he sees a wolf coming, and leave the sheep, for they aren't his and he isn't their shepherd. And so the wolf leaps on them and scatters the flock. The hired man runs because he is hired and has no real concern for the sheep.

"I am the Good Shepherd and know My own sheep, and they know Me, just as My Father knows Me and I know the Father; and I lay down My life for the sheep. I have other sheep, too, in another fold. I must bring them also, and they will heed My voice; and there will be one flock with one Shepherd.

"The Father loves Me because I lay down My life that I may have it back again. No one can kill Me without My consent—I lay down My life voluntarily. For I have the right and power to lay it down when I want to and also the right and power to take it again. For the Father has given Me this right."

John 10:6-18

When He said these things, the Jewish leaders were again divided in their opinions about Him. Some of them said, "He has a demon or else is crazy. Why listen to a man like that?"

Others said, "This doesn't sound to us like a man possessed by a demon! Can a demon open the eyes of blind men?"

The Lord chose 70 other disciples and sent them on ahead in pairs to all the towns and villages He planned to visit later. These were His instructions to them: "Plead with the Lord of the harvest to send out more laborers to help you, for the harvest is so plentiful and the workers so few! Go now, and remember that I am sending you out as lambs among wolves! Don't take any money with you, or a beggar's bag, or even an extra pair of shoes. And don't waste time along the way.

"Whenever you enter a home, give it your blessing. If it is worthy of the blessing, the blessing will stand; if not, the blessing will return to you. When you enter a village, don't shift around from home to home; but stay in one place, eating and drinking without question whatever is set before you. And don't hesitate to accept hospitality, for the workman is worthy of his wages!

"If a town welcomes you, follow these two rules: (1) Eat whatever is set before you. (2) Heal the sick; and as you heal them, say, 'The Kingdom of God is very near you now.'

"But if a town refuses you, go out into its streets

John 10:19-21; Luke 10:1-10

and say, 'We wipe the dust of your town from our feet as a public announcement of your doom. Never forget how close you were to the Kingdom of God!' Even wicked Sodom will be better off than such a city on the Judgment Day.

"What horrors await you, you cities of Chorazin and Bethsaida! For if the miracles I did for you had been done in the cities of Tyre and Sidon, their people would have sat in deep repentance long ago, clothed in sackcloth and throwing ashes on their heads to show their remorse. Yes, Tyre and Sidon will receive less punishment on the Judgment Day than you. And you people of Capernaum, what shall I say about you? Will you be exalted to heaven? No, you shall be brought down to hell."

Then He said to the disciples, "Those who welcome you are welcoming Me. And those who reject you are rejecting Me. And those who reject Me are rejecting God, who sent Me."

When the 70 disciples returned, they joyfully reported to Him, "Even the demons obey us when we use Your name."

"Yes," He told them, "I saw Satan falling from heaven as a flash of lightning! And I have given you authority over all the power of the Enemy, and to walk among serpents and scorpions and to crush them! Nothing shall injure you! However, the important thing is not that demons obey you, but that your names are registered as citizens of heaven!"

Then He was filled with the joy of the Holy

Luke 10:10-21

Spirit and said, "I praise You, O Father, Lord of heaven and earth, for hiding these things from the intellectuals—the worldly wise—and for revealing them to those who are as trusting as little children. Yes, thank You, Father, for that is the way You wanted it. I am the Agent of My Father in everything; and no one except the Father really knows the Son, and no one knows the Father except the Son and those to whom the Son chooses to show Him.

"Come to Me and I will give you rest—all of you who work so hard beneath a heavy yoke. Wear My yoke—for it fits perfectly—and let Me teach you; for I am gentle and humble, and you shall find rest for your souls; for I give you only light burdens."

Then, turning to the twelve disciples, He said quietly, "How privileged you are to see what you have seen! Many a prophet and king of old has longed for these days; to see and hear what you have seen and heard!"

Luke 10:21,22; Matthew 11:28-30; Luke 10:23,24

Chapter 24

Help on the Highway

One day an expert on Moses' laws came to test Jesus' orthodoxy by asking Him this question: "Teacher, what does a man need to do to live forever in heaven?"

Jesus replied, "What does Moses' law say about it?"

"It says," he replied, "that you must love the Lord your God with all your heart, and with all your soul, and with all your strength, and with all your mind. And you must love your neighbor just as much as you love yourself."

"Right!" Jesus told him. "Do this and you shall live!"

The man wanted to justify his lack of love for some kinds of people, so he asked, "Which neighbors?"

Jesus replied with an illustration: "A Jew going on a trip from Jerusalem to Jericho was attacked by bandits. They stripped him of his clothes and money and beat him up and left him lying half dead beside the road. By chance a Jewish priest came along; and though he saw the man lying there, he crossed to the other side of the road and went by. A Jewish Temple-assistant did the same thing; he, too, left him lying there.

"But a despised Samaritan came along; and when

Luke 10:25-33

he saw him, he felt deep pity for him. Kneeling beside him, the Samaritan soothed his wounds with medicine and bandaged them. Then he put the man on his donkey and walked along beside him till they came to an inn. He nursed him through the night, and the next day he handed the innkeeper two twenty-dollar bills and told him to take care of the man. 'If his bill runs higher than that,' he said, 'I'll pay the difference the next time I am here.'

"Now which of these three would you say was a neighbor to the bandits' victim?"

The man replied, "The one who showed him some pity."

Then Jesus said, "Yes, now go and do the same."

As Jesus and the disciples continued on their way, they came to a village where a woman named Martha welcomed them into her home. Her sister Mary sat spellbound on the floor, listening to Jesus as He talked. But Martha was the jittery type, and was worrying over the big dinner she was preparing. She came to Jesus and said, "Sir, doesn't it seem unfair to You that my sister just sits there while I do all the work? Make her come and help me."

But the Lord said to her, "Martha, dear friend, you are so upset over all these details! There is really only one thing worth your concern. Mary has chosen it—and I won't take it away from her!"

Once when Jesus had been out praying, one of His disciples came to Him as He finished and said,

Luke 10:33-42; Luke 11:1

"Lord, teach us a prayer to recite like the one John taught his disciples."

And this is the prayer He taught them: "Father, may Your name be honored for its holiness; send Your Kingdom soon! Give us our food day by day, and forgive our sins—for we have forgiven those who sinned against us. And don't allow us to be tempted."

Then, teaching them more about prayer, He used this illustration: "Suppose you went to a friend's house at midnight, wanting to borrow three loaves of bread! You would shout to him, 'A friend of mine has just arrived for a visit and I've nothing to give him to eat.' He would call down from his bedroom, 'Please don't ask me to get up! The door is locked for the night and we are all in bed. I just can't help you this time!'

"But I'll tell you this—though he won't do it as a friend, if you keep knocking long enough he will get up and give you everything you want—just because of your persistence! And so it is with prayer—keep on asking, and you will keep on getting; keep on looking, and you will keep on finding; knock, and the door will be opened! Everyone who asks, receives; all who seek, find; and the door is opened to everyone who knocks.

"You men who are fathers—if your boy asks for bread, do you give him a stone? If he asks for fish, do you give him a snake? If he asks for an egg, does he get a scorpion from you? Of course not! And if

Luke 11:1-12

even sinful persons like yourselves give children what they need, don't you realize that your heavenly Father will do at least as much, and give the Holy Spirit to those who ask for Him?"

Once when Jesus cast out a demon from a man who couldn't speak, his voice returned to him again. Most of the crowd was enthusiastic, but some said, "No wonder He can cast them out. He gets His power from Satan, the king of demons!" Others asked for something to happen in the sky to prove His claim of being the Messiah.

He knew the thoughts of each of them, so He said, "Any kingdom filled with civil war is doomed, so is a home filled with argument and strife. Therefore, if Satan is fighting against himself by empowering Me to cast out his demons, as you are saying, how can his kingdom survive?

"And if I am empowered by Satan, what about your own followers? For they cast out demons! Do you think this proves they are possessed by Satan? Ask them if you are right! But if I am casting out demons because of power from God, it proves that the Kingdom of God has arrived! For when Satan, strong and full-armed, guards his palace, it is safe—until someone stronger and better armed attacks and overcomes him and strips him of his weapons and carries off his belongings! Anyone who is not for Me is against Me; if he isn't helping Me, he is hurting My cause.

"When a demon is cast out of a man, it goes to

Luke 11:13-2

the deserts, searching there for rest; but finding none, it returns to the person it left and finds its former home all swept and clean. Then it goes and gets seven other demons more evil than itself, and they all enter the man. And so the poor fellow is seven times worse off than he was before."

As He was speaking, a woman in the crowd called out, "God bless Your mother—the womb from which You came, and the breasts that gave You suck!"

He replied, "Yes, but even more blessed are all who hear the Word of God and put it into practice."

As the crowd pressed in upon Him, He preached them this sermon: "These are evil times, with evil people. They keep asking for some strange happening in the skies to prove I am the Messiah, but the only proof I will give them is a miracle like that of Jonah, whose experiences proved to the people of Nineveh that God had sent him. My similar experience will prove that God has sent Me to these people.

"And at the Judgment Day the Queen of Sheba shall arise and point her finger at this generation, condemning it, for she went on a long, hard journey to listen to the wisdom of Solomon; but one far greater than Solomon is here and the people pay no attention. The men of Nineveh, too, shall arise and condemn this nation, for they repented at the

Luke 11:24-32

preaching of Jonah; and someone far greater than Jonah is here and it won't listen.

"No one lights a lamp and hides it! Instead he puts it on a lampstand to give light to all who enter the room. Your eye lights up your inward being. A pure eye lets sunshine into your soul. A lustful eye shuts out the light and plunges you into darkness. So watch out that the sunshine isn't blotted out. If you are filled with light within, with no dark corners, then the outside will be radiant too, as though a floodlight is beamed upon you."

Luke 11:32-36

Chapter 25

Why Worry?

As He was speaking, one of the Pharisees asked Him home for a meal. When Jesus arrived, He sat down to eat without first performing the ceremonial washing required by Jewish custom. This greatly surprised His host. Then Jesus said to him, "You Pharisees wash the outside, but inside you are still unclean—full of greed and wickedness! Fools! Didn't God make the inside as well as the outside? Purity is best demonstrated by generosity!

"But woe to you, Pharisees! For though you are careful to tithe even the smallest part of your income, you completely forget about justice and the love of God. You should tithe, yes, but you should not leave these other things undone!

"Woe to you, Pharisees! For how you love the seats of honor in the synagogues and respectful greetings from everyone as you walk through the markets! Yes, awesome judgment is resting upon you! For you are like hidden graves in a field. Men pass by you with no knowledge of the corruption nearby."

"Sir," said an expert in religious law who was standing there, "You have insulted my profession, too, in what You just said."

"Yes," said Jesus, "the same horrors await you!

Luke 11:37-46

For you crush men beneath impossible religious demands—demands that you yourselves would never think of trying to keep! Woe to you! For you are exactly like your ancestors who killed the prophets long ago. Murderers! You agree with your fathers that what they did was right—you would have done the same yourselves.

"This is what God says about you: 'I will send prophets and apostles to you, and you will kill some of them and chase away the others'; and you of this generation will be held responsible for the murder of God's servants from the founding of the world—from the murder of Abel to the murder of Zechariah who perished between the altar and the sanctuary. Yes, it will surely be charged against you.

"Woe to you, experts in religion! For you hide the truth from the people; you won't accept it for yourselves, and you prevent others from having a chance to believe it."

The Pharisees and legal experts were furious; and from that time on they plied Him fiercely with a host of questions, trying to trap Him into saying something for which they could have Him arrested.

The crowds that followed Him grew until thousands upon thousands were milling about and crushing each other. He turned now to His disciples and warned them, "More than anything else, beware of these Pharisees and the way they pretend to be good when they aren't. But such hypocrisy cannot be hidden forever. Though they conceal it

Luke 11:46-54; Luke 12:1,2

now, it will be exposed. And for you also it is true that whatever you have said in the dark shall be heard in the light, and what you have whispered in the inner rooms shall be broadcast from the housetops for all to hear!

"Dear friends, don't be afraid of these who want to murder you! They can only kill the body; they have no power over your souls. But I'll tell you whom to fear—fear God who has the power to kill and then cast into hell.

"What is the price of five sparrows? A couple of pennies? Not much more than that! Yet God does not forget a single one of them. And He knows the number of hairs on your head! Never fear, you are far more valuable to Him than a whole flock of sparrows!

"And I assure you of this: I, the Son of Man, will publicly honor you in the presence of God's angels if you publicly acknowledge Me here on earth as your Friend. But I will deny before the angels those who deny Me here among men. Yet those who speak against Me may be forgiven—while those who speak against the Holy Spirit shall never be forgiven.

"And when you are brought to trial before these Jewish rulers and authorities in the synagogues, don't be concerned about what to say in your defense, for the Holy Spirit will give you the right words even as you stand there."

Then someone called from the crowd, "Sir, please

Luke 12:2-12

tell my brother to divide my father's estate with me."

But Jesus replied, "Man, who made Me a judge over you to decide things like that? Beware! Don't always be wishing for what others have."

Then He gave an illustration: "A rich man had a fertile farm that produced fine crops. In fact, his barns were full to overflowing—he couldn't get everything in. He thought about his problem and finally exclaimed, 'I know—I'll tear down my barns and build bigger ones! Then I'll have room enough! And I'll sit back and say to myself, "Friend, you have enough stored away for years to come. Now take it easy! Wine, women and song for you!"' But God said to him, 'Fool! Tonight you die. Then who will get it all?'

"Yes, every man is a fool who gets rich on earth but not in heaven."

Then turning to His disciples He said, "Don't worry about whether you have enough food to eat or clothes to wear. For life consists of far more than food and clothes. Look at the ravens—they don't plant or harvest or have barns to store away their food, and yet they get along all right—for God feeds them. And you are far more valuable to Him than birds!

"And besides, what's the use of worrying? What good does it do? Will it add a single day to your life? Of course not. And if it can't even do little things like that, what's the use of worrying over

Luke 12:12-25

bigger things? Look at the lilies! They don't toil and spin, and yet Solomon in all his glory was not robed as well as they are. And if God provides clothing for the flowers that are here today and gone tomorrow—don't you suppose He will provide clothing for you, you doubters?

"And don't worry about food—what to eat and drink; don't worry at all that God will provide it for you. All mankind scratches for its daily bread. But your heavenly Father knows your needs. He will always give you all you need from day to day if you will make the Kingdom of God your primary concern. So don't be afraid, little flock. For it gives your Father great happiness to give you the Kingdom.

"Sell what you have and give to those in need. This will fatten your purses in heaven! And the purses of heaven have no rips or holes in them! Your treasures there will never disappear; no thief can steal them; no moth can destroy them! Wherever your treasure is, there your heart and thoughts will be also!

"Be prepared—all dressed and ready—for your Lord's return from the wedding feast. Then you will be ready to open the door and let Him in the moment He arrives and knocks. There will be great joy for those who are ready and waiting for His return. He, Himself, will seat them and put on a waiter's uniform and serve them as they sit and eat! He may come at nine o'clock at night—or even at

Luke 12:25-37

midnight. But whenever He comes, there will be joy for His servants who are ready!

"Everyone would be ready for Him if they knew the exact hour of His return—just as they would be ready for a thief if they knew when he was coming! So be ready all the time! For I, the Son of Man, will come when least expected."

Peter asked, "Lord, are You talking just to us or to everyone?"

And the Lord replied, "I'm talking to any faithful, sensible man whose master gives him the responsibility of feeding the other servants regularly. If his master returns and finds that his servant has done a good job, there will be a reward—his master will put him in charge of all he owns.

"But if the man begins to think, 'My lord won't be back for a long time,' and begins to whip the men and women he is supposed to protect, and spends his time at drinking parties and in drunkenness—well, his master will return without notice and remove him from his position of trust and assign him to the place of the unfaithful. He will be severely punished, for though he knew his duty, he refused to do it. But anyone who is not aware that he is doing wrong will be punished only lightly. Much is required from those to whom much is given, for their responsibility is greater.

"I have come to bring fire to the earth, and, oh, that My task were completed! There is a terrible baptism ahead of Me, and how I am pent up until

Luke 12:37-49

it is accomplished! Do you think I have come to give peace to the earth? No! Rather, strife and division! From now on families will be split apart, three in favor of Me, and two against Me—or perhaps the other way around. A father will decide one way about Me; his son, the other; mother and daughter will disagree; and the decision of an honored mother-in-law will be spurned by her daughter-in-law."

Then He turned to the crowd and said, "When you see clouds beginning to form in the west, you say, 'Here comes a shower.' And you are right. When the south wind blows, you say, 'Today will be a scorcher.' And it is. Hypocrites! You interpret the sky well enough, but you refuse to notice the warnings all around you about crises ahead. Why do you refuse to see for yourselves what is right?

"If you meet your accuser on the way to court, try to settle the matter before it reaches the judge, lest he sentence you to jail; in which case you won't be free again until the last penny is paid in full."

Luke 12:49-59

Chapter 26

Disputed Claims

One time He was informed that Pilate had butchered some Jews from Galilee as they were sacrificing at the Temple in Jerusalem. "Do you think they were worse sinners than other men from Galilee?" He asked. "Is that why they suffered? No! Don't you know that you also will perish unless you leave your evil way and turn to God?

"And what about the 18 men who died when the tower of Siloam fell on them? Were they the worst sinners in Jerusalem? No! You will perish, too, unless you repent."

Then He used this illustration: "A man planted a fig tree in his garden and came again and again to see if he could find any fruit on it, but he was always disappointed. Finally he told his gardener to cut it down. 'I've waited three years and have not found a single fig!' he said. 'Why bother with it any longer? It's taking up space we can use for something else.' 'Give it one more chance,' the gardener answered. 'Leave it another year, and I'll give it special attention and plenty of fertilizer. If we get figs next year, fine; if not, I'll cut it down.'"

One Sabbath as He was teaching in a synagogue,

Luke 13:1-10

He saw a seriously handicapped woman who had been bent double for 18 years and was unable to straighten herself and stand upright. Calling her over to Him, Jesus said, "Woman, you are healed of your sickness!" He touched her, and instantly she could stand straight! How she praised and thanked God!

But the local Jewish leader in charge of the synagogue was very angry about it because Jesus had healed her on the Sabbath day. "There are six days of the week to work," he shouted to the crowd. "Those are the days to come for healing, not on the Sabbath!"

But the Lord replied, "You hypocrites! You work on the Sabbath! Don't you untie your cattle from their stalls on the Sabbath and lead them out for water? And is it wrong for Me, just because it is the Sabbath day, to free this Jewish woman from Satan's 18 years of bondage?"

This shamed His enemies. But the rest of the people rejoiced at the wonderful things He did.

Now He began teaching them again about the Kingdom of God: "What is the Kingdom like?" He asked. "How can I illustrate it? It is like a tiny mustard seed planted in a garden; soon it grows into a tall bush, and the birds live among its branches ... It is like yeast kneaded into dough, which works unseen until it has risen high and light."

Luke 13:11-21

December, A.D. 29

It was winter, and Jesus was in Jerusalem at the time of the Dedication Celebration. He was at the Temple, walking through the section known as Solomon's Cloister.

The Jewish leaders surrounded Him and asked, "How long are You going to keep us in suspense? If you are the Messiah, tell us plainly."

"I have already told you, and you didn't believe Me," Jesus replied. "The proof is in the miracles I do in the name of My Father. But you don't believe Me because you are not part of My flock. My sheep recognize My voice, and I know them, and they follow Me. I give them eternal life, and they shall never perish. No one shall snatch them away from Me, for My Father has given them to Me, and He is more powerful than anyone else, so no one can kidnap them from Me. I and the Father are one."

Then again the Jewish leaders picked up stones to kill Him.

Jesus said, "At God's direction I have done many a miracle to help the people. For which one are you killing Me?"

They replied, "Not for any good work, but for blasphemy; You, a mere man, have declared Yourself to be God."

"In your own Law it says that men are gods!" He replied. "So if the Scripture which cannot be untrue speaks of those as gods, to whom the message of

John 10:22-35

God came, do you call it blasphemy when the one sanctified and sent into the world by the Father says, 'I am the Son of God'? Don't believe Me unless I do miracles of God. But if I do, believe them even if you don't believe Me! Then you will become convinced that the Father is in Me, and I in the Father."

January, A.D. 30

Once again they started to arrest Him. But He walked away and left them and went beyond the Jordan River to stay near the place where John was first baptizing. And many followed Him. "John didn't do miracles," they remarked to one another, "but all his predictions concerning this man have come true." And many came to the decision that He was the Messiah.

He went from city to city and village to village, teaching as He went, always pressing onward toward Jerusalem. Someone asked Him, "Will only a few be saved?"

And He replied, "The door to heaven is narrow. Work hard to get in, for the truth is, many will try to enter, but when the head of the house has locked the door, it will be too late. Then if you stand outside knocking and pleading, 'Lord, open the door for us,' He will reply, 'I do not know you.' 'But we ate with You, and You taught in our streets,' you will say. And He will reply, 'I tell you, I don't

John 10:35-42; Luke 13:22-27

know you. You can't come in here, guilty as you are. Go away.'

"And there will be great weeping and gnashing of teeth as you stand outside and see Abraham, Isaac, Jacob and all the prophets within the Kingdom of God—for people will come from all over the world to take their places in the Kingdom of God. And note this: Some who are despised now will be greatly honored then; and some who are highly thought of now will be least important then."

A few minutes later some Pharisees said to Him, "Get out of here if You want to live, for King Herod is after You!"

"Go tell that fox," Jesus said, "that I will keep on casting out demons and doing miracles of healing today and tomorrow; and the third day I will reach my destination. Yes, today, tomorrow, and the next day! For it wouldn't do for a prophet of God to be killed except in Jerusalem!"

Luke 13:27-33

Chapter 27

Stories with Barbs

One Sabbath as He was in the home of one of the Jewish council members, the Pharisees were watching Him like hawks to see if He would heal a man who was present, suffering from dropsy. Jesus said to the Pharisees and legal experts standing around, "Well, is it within the Law to heal a man on the Sabbath day, or not?" And when they refused to answer, Jesus took the sick man by the hand and healed him and sent him away.

Then He turned to them, "Which of you doesn't work on the Sabbath? If your cow falls into a pit, don't you proceed to get it out at once?" Again they had no answer.

When He noticed that everyone who came to the dinner was trying to sit near the head of the table, He gave them this advice: "If you are invited to a wedding feast, don't always head for the best seat. For if someone more respected than you shows up, the host will bring him to your place and say, 'Let this man sit here instead.' And you, embarrassed, will have to take whatever seat is left at the foot of the table!

"Do this instead—start at the foot; and when your host sees you, he will come and say, 'Friend, we have a better place than this for you!' Thus you

Luke 14:1-10

will be honored in front of all the other guests! For everyone who tries to honor himself shall be humbled; and he who humbles himself shall be honored."

Then He turned to His host. "When you put on a dinner," He said, "don't invite friends, brothers, relatives and rich neighbors! For they will return the invitation! Instead, invite the poor, the crippled, the lame and the blind. Then at the resurrection of the godly, God will reward you for inviting those who can't repay you."

Hearing this, a man sitting at the table with Jesus exclaimed, "What a privilege it would be to get into the Kingdom of God!"

But Jesus replied with this illustration: "A man prepared a great feast and invited many to come. When all was ready, he sent his servant around to notify the guests that it was time for them to come. But then they all began making excuses. One said he had just bought a field and wanted to inspect it, and he asked to be excused. Another said he had just bought five pair of oxen and wanted to try them out. Another had just been married and for that reason couldn't come.

"The servant returned and reported to his master what they had said. His master was angry and told him to go quickly into the streets and alleys of the city and to invite the beggars, crippled, lame and blind. But even after he had done this, there was still room! 'Well then,' said his master, 'go out into

Luke 14:10-23

the country lanes and out behind the hedges and urge anyone you find to come, so that the house will be full. For none of those I invited first will get even the smallest taste of what I had prepared for them.' "

Great crowds were following Him. He turned around and addressed them as follows: "Anyone who wants to be My follower must love Me far more than he does his own father, mother, wife, children, brothers or sisters—yes, more than his own life—otherwise he cannot be My disciple. And no one can be My disciple who does not carry his own cross and follow Me.

"But don't begin until you count the cost. For who would begin construction of a building without first getting estimates and then checking to see if he has enough money to pay the bills? Otherwise he might only complete the foundation before running out of funds. And then how everyone would laugh! 'See that fellow there?' they would mock. 'He started that building and ran out of money before it was finished!'

"Or what king would ever dream of going to war without sitting down first with his counselors and discussing whether his army of 10,000 is strong enough to defeat the 20,000 men who are marching against him? If the decision is negative, then while the enemy troops are still far away, he will send a truce team to discuss terms of peace. So no one can become My disciple unless he first sits down and

Luke 14:23-33

counts his blessings—and then renounces them all for Me!

"What good is salt that has lost its saltiness? Flavorless salt is fit for nothing—not even for fertilizer. It is worthless and must be thrown out. Listen well, if you would understand My meaning."

Dishonest tax collectors and other notorious sinners were all gathering to listen to Jesus' sermons; and the Jewish religious leaders and the experts on Jewish law complained because He was associating with such people—even eating with them!

So Jesus used this illustration: "If you had 100 sheep and one of them strayed away and was lost in the wilderness, wouldn't you leave the 99 others to go and search for the lost one until you found it? And then you would joyfully carry it home on your shoulders. When you arrived you would call together your friends and neighbors to rejoice with you because your lost sheep was found. Well, in the same way heaven will be happier over the one lost sinner who returns to God than over the 99 others who haven't strayed away!

"Or take another illustration: A woman has ten valuable silver coins and loses one. Won't she light a lamp and look in every corner of the house and sweep every nook and cranny until she finds it? And then won't she call in her friends and neighbors to rejoice with her? In the same way there is joy in the presence of the angels of God when one sinner repents."

Luke 14:33-35; Luke 15:1-10

To further illustrate the point, He told them this story: "A man has two sons. When the younger told his father, 'I want my share of your estate now, instead of waiting until you die!' his father agreed to divide his wealth between his sons.

"A few days later this younger son packed all his belongings and took a trip to a distant land, and there wasted all his money on parties and prostitutes. About the time his money was gone, a great famine swept over the land, and he began to starve. He persuaded a local farmer to hire him, and the farmer sent him out into the fields to feed pigs. But even so, the boy became so hungry he gladly would have eaten the pods he was feeding the swine. And no one gave him anything.

"When he finally came to his senses, he said to himself, 'At home even the hired men have food enough and to spare, and here I am, dying of hunger! I will go home to my father and say, "Father, I have sinned against both heaven and you, and am no longer worthy of being called your son. Please take me on as a hired man." '

"So he returned home to his father. And while he was still a long distance away, his father saw him coming and was filled with loving pity and ran and embraced him and kissed him. His son said to him, 'Father, I have sinned against heaven and you, and am not worthy of being called your son . . .' But his father said to the slaves, 'Quick! Bring the finest robe in the house and put it on him. And a jeweled

Luke 15:10-22

ring for his finger; and shoes! And kill the calf we have in the fattening pen. We must celebrate with a feast, for this son of mine was dead and has returned to life! He was lost and is found!' So the party began.

"Meanwhile the older son was in the fields working; when he returned home, he heard dance music coming from the house. He asked one of the servants what was going on. 'Your brother is back,' he was told, 'and your father has killed the calf we were fattening and has prepared a great feast to celebrate his coming home again unharmed.'

"The older brother was angry and wouldn't go in. His father came out and begged him, but he replied, 'All these years I've worked hard for you and never once refused to do a single thing you told me to; and in all that time you never gave me even one young goat for a feast with my friends. Yet when this son of yours comes back after spending your money on prostitutes, you celebrate by killing the finest calf we have on the place.'

" 'Look, son, dear,' his father said to him, 'you and I are very close, and everything I have is yours. But it is right to celebrate. For he is your brother; and he was dead and has come back to life! He was lost and is found!' "

Jesus told this story to His disciples: "A rich man hired an accountant to handle his affairs, but soon a rumor went around that the accountant was thoroughly dishonest. So his employer called him in and

Luke 15:22-32; Luke 16:1,2

said, 'What's this I hear about your stealing from me? Get your report in order, for you are to be dismissed.' The accountant thought to himself, 'Now what? I'm through here, and I haven't the strength to go out and dig ditches, and I'm too proud to beg. I know just the thing! And then I'll have plenty of friends to take care of me when I leave!'

"So he invited each one who owed money to his employer to come and discuss the matter with him. He asked the first one, 'How much do you owe him?' 'My debt is 850 gallons of olive oil,' the man answered. 'Here is your agreement to pay him 850 gallons,' the accountant told him. 'Tear it up and write another one for half that much!'

"'And how much do you owe him?' he asked the next man. 'A thousand bushels of wheat,' was the reply. 'Here,' the accountant said, 'take your note and replace it with one for only 800 bushels!' The rich man had to admire the rascal for being so shrewd. And it was true that the citizens of this world are more clever in dishonesty than the godly are.

"But shall I tell you to act that way to buy friendship through cheating? Will this ensure your entry into an everlasting home in heaven? No! For unless you are honest in small matters, you won't be in large. If you cheat even a little, you won't be honest with greater responsibilities. And if you are untrustworthy about worldly wealth, who will trust

Luke 16:2-12

you with the true riches of heaven? And if you are not faithful with other people's money, why should you be entrusted with money of your own?

"For neither you nor anyone else can serve two masters. You will hate one and show loyalty to the other, or else, the other way around—be enthusiastic about one and despise the other. You cannot serve both God and money."

The Pharisees, who dearly loved their money, naturally scoffed at all this. Then He said to them, "You wear a noble, pious expression in public, but God knows your evil hearts. Your pretense brings you honor from the people, but it is an abomination in the sight of God. Until John the Baptist began to preach, the Old Testament laws and the messages of the prophets were your guides. But John introduced the Good News that the Kingdom of God would come soon. And now eager multitudes are pressing in. But that doesn't mean the Law has lost its force in even the smallest point. It is as strong and unshakable as heaven and earth. So anyone who divorces his wife and marries someone else commits adultery, and anyone who marries a divorced woman commits adultery."

"There was a certain rich man," Jesus said, "who was splendidly clothed and lived each day in mirth and luxury. One day Lazarus, a diseased beggar, was laid at his door. As he lay there longing for scraps from the rich man's table, the dogs would come and lick his open sores. Finally the beggar

Luke 16:12-22

died and was carried by the angels to be with Abraham in the place of the righteous dead. The rich man also died and was buried. And his soul went into hell. There, in torment, he saw Lazarus in the far distance with Abraham.

"'Father Abraham,' he shouted, 'have some pity. Send Lazarus over here if only to dip the tip of his finger in water and cool my tongue, for I am in anguish in these flames.' But Abraham said to him, 'Son, remember that during your lifetime you had everything you wanted, and Lazarus had nothing. So now he is here being comforted and you are in anguish. And besides, there is a great chasm separating us, and anyone wanting to come to you from here is stopped at its edge; and no one over there can cross to us.'

"Then the rich man said, 'O Father Abraham, then please send him to my father's home—for I have five brothers—to warn them about this place of torment so that they won't come here when they die.'

"But Abraham said, "The Scriptures have warned them again and again. Your brothers can read them any time they want to.'

"The rich man replied, 'No, Father Abraham, they won't bother to read them. But if someone is sent to them from the dead, then they will turn from their sins.'

"Then Abraham said, 'If they won't listen to

Luke 16:22-31

Moses and the prophets, they won't listen even if someone rises from the dead.' "

"There will always be temptations to sin," Jesus said one day to His disciples, "but woe to the man who does the tempting. If he were thrown into the sea with a huge rock tied to his neck, he would be far better off than facing the punishment in store for those who harm these little children's souls. I am warning you! Rebuke your brother if he sins, and forgive him if he is sorry. Even if he wrongs you seven times every day and each time turns again and asks forgiveness, forgive him."

One day the apostles said to the Lord, "We need more faith; tell us how to get it."

"If your faith were only the size of a mustard seed," Jesus answered, "it would be large enough to uproot that mulberry tree over there and send it hurtling into the sea! Your command would bring immediate results! When a servant comes in from plowing or taking care of sheep, he doesn't just sit down and eat, but first prepares his master's meal and serves him his supper before he eats his own. And he is not even thanked, for he is merely doing what he is supposed to do! Just so, if you merely obey Me, you should not consider yourselves worthy of praise! For you have simply done your duty!"

Luke 17:1-10

Chapter 28

Beyond Hope?

February, A.D. 30

Do you remember Mary, who poured the costly perfume on Jesus' feet and wiped them with her hair? Well, her brother Lazarus, who lived in Bethany with his sisters Mary and Martha, was sick. So the two sisters sent a message to Jesus telling Him, "Sir, your good friend is very, very sick."

But when Jesus heard about it, He said, "The purpose of his illness is not death, but for the glory of God. I, the Son of God, will receive glory from this situation." Although Jesus was very fond of Martha, Mary and Lazarus, He stayed where He was for the next two days and made no move to go to them.

Finally, after the two days, He said to His disciples, "Let's go to Judea."

But His disciples objected. "Master," they said, "only a few days ago the Jewish leaders in Judea were trying to kill You. Are You going there again?"

Jesus replied, "There are 12 hours of daylight every day, and during every hour of it a man can walk safely and not stumble. Only at night is there danger of a wrong step, because of the dark."

John 11:1-10

Then He said, "Our friend Lazarus has gone to sleep, but now I will go and waken him!"

The disciples, thinking Jesus meant Lazarus was having a good night's rest, said, "That means he is getting better!"

But Jesus meant Lazarus had died. Then He told them plainly, "Lazarus is dead. And for your sake, I am glad I wasn't there, for this will give you another opportunity to believe in Me. Come, let's go to him."

Thomas, nicknamed "The Twin," said to his fellow disciples, "Let's go too—and die with Him."

When they arrived at Bethany, they were told that Lazarus had already been in his tomb for four days! Bethany was only a couple of miles down the road from Jerusalem and many of the Jewish leaders had come to pay their respects and to console Martha and Mary on their loss.

When Martha got word that Jesus was coming, she went to meet Him. But Mary stayed at home. Martha said to Jesus, "Sir, if You had been here, my brother wouldn't have died. And even now it's not too late, for I know that God will bring my brother back to life again, if You will only ask Him to."

Jesus told her, "Your brother will come back to life again."

"Yes," Martha said, "when everyone else does, on Resurrection Day."

Jesus told her, "I am the one who raises the dead and gives them life again. Anyone who believes in

John 11:11-25

Me, even though he dies like anyone else, shall live again. He is given eternal life for believing in Me and shall never perish. Do you believe this, Martha?"

"Yes, Master," she told Him. "I believe You are the Messiah, the Son of God, the one we have so long awaited." Then she left Him and returned to Mary and calling her aside from the mourners told her, "He is here and wants to see you." Mary left immediately to go to Him.

Now Jesus had stayed outside the village, at the place where Martha met Him. When the Jewish leaders who were at the house trying to console Mary saw her hastily leave, they assumed she was going to Lazarus' tomb to weep; so they followed her. When Mary arrived where Jesus was, she fell down at His feet, saying, "Sir, if You had been here, my brother would still be alive."

When Jesus saw her weeping and the Jewish leaders wailing with her, He was moved with indignation and deeply troubled. "Where is he buried?" He asked them.

They told Him, "Come and see."

Tears came to Jesus' eyes. "They were close friends," the Jewish leaders said. "See how much He loved him." But some said, "This fellow healed a blind man—why couldn't He keep Lazarus from dying?" And again Jesus was moved with deep anger. Then they came to the tomb. It was a cave with a heavy stone rolled across its door.

John 11:25-38

"Roll the stone aside," Jesus told them.

But Martha, the dead man's sister, said, "By now the smell will be terrible, for he has been dead four days."

"But didn't I tell you that you will see a wonderful miracle from God if you believe?" Jesus asked her.

So they rolled the stone aside. Then Jesus looked up to heaven and said, "Father, thank You for hearing Me. You always hear Me, of course, but I said it because of all these people standing here, so that they will believe You sent Me."

Then He shouted, "Lazarus, come out!"

And Lazarus came—bound up in the gravecloth, his face muffled in a head swath. Jesus told them, "Unwrap him and let him go!"

And so at last many of the Jewish leaders who were with Mary and saw it happen, finally believed on Him! But some went away to the Pharisees and reported it to them.

Then the chief priests and Pharisees convened a council to discuss the situation. "What are we going to do?" they asked each other, "for this man certainly does miracles. If we let Him alone, the whole nation will follow Him—and then the Roman army will come and kill us and take over the Jewish government."

But one of them, Caiaphas, who was High Priest that year, said, "You stupid idiots—let this one man

John 11:39-50

die for the people—why should the whole nation perish?"

This prophecy that Jesus should die for the entire nation came from Caiaphas in his position as High Priest—he didn't think of it by himself, but was inspired to say it. It was a prediction that Jesus' death would not be for Israel only, but for all the children of God scattered around the world.

So from that time on the Jewish leaders began plotting Jesus' death.

Jesus now stopped His public ministry and left Jerusalem; He went to the edge of the desert to the village of Ephraim and stayed there with His disciples.

March, A.D. 30

Sometime later as they continued onward toward Jerusalem, they reached the border between Galilee and Samaria and entered a village. Ten lepers stood at a distance crying out, "Jesus, Sir, have mercy on us!"

He glanced at them and said, "Go to the Jewish priest and show him that you are healed!" And as they were on their way, their leprosy disappeared!

One of them came back to Jesus, shouting, "Glory to God, I am healed!" He fell flat on the ground in front of Jesus, face downward in the dust, thanking Him for what He had done. This man was a despised Samaritan.

John 11:50-54; Luke 17:11-16

Jesus asked, "Didn't I heal ten men? Where are the nine? Does only this foreigner return to give glory to God?" And Jesus said to the man, "Stand up and go; your faith has made you well."

Luke 17:17-19

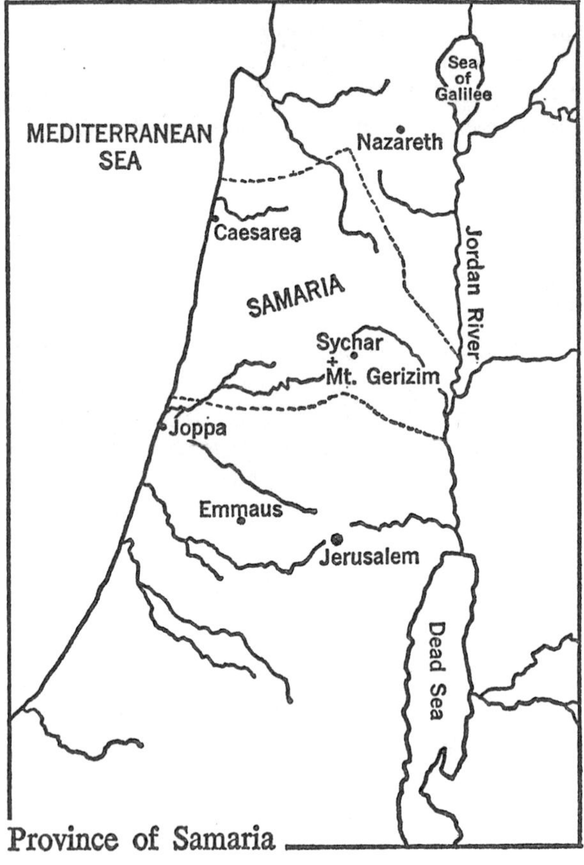

Province of Samaria

Chapter 29

Patterns for Living

One day the Pharisees asked Jesus, "When will the Kingdom of God begin?" Jesus replied, "The Kingdom of God isn't ushered in with visible signs! You won't be able to say, 'It has begun here in this place or there in that part of the country.' For the Kingdom of God is within you."

Later He talked about this again with His disciples. "The time is coming when you will long for Me to be with you even for a single day, but I won't be here," He said.

One day Jesus told His disciples a story to illustrate their need for constant prayer and to show them that they must keep praying until the answer comes!

"There was a city judge," He said, "a very godless man, who had great contempt for everyone. A widow of that city came to him frequently to appeal for justice against a man who had harmed her. The judge ignored her for a while, but eventually she got on his nerves. 'I fear neither God nor man,' he said to himself, 'but this woman bothers me. I'm going to see that she gets justice, for she is wearing me out with her constant nagging!' "

Then the Lord said, "If even an evil judge can be worn down like that, don't you think that God will

Luke 17:20-22; Luke 18:1-7

surely give justice to His people who plead with Him day and night? Yes! He will answer them quickly! But the question is: When I, the Son of Man, return, how many will I find who have faith and are praying?"

Then He told this story to some who boasted of their virtue and scorned everyone else: "Two men went to the Temple to pray. One was a proud, self-righteous Pharisee, and the other a cheating tax collector. The proud Pharisee 'prayed' this prayer: 'Thank God, I am not a sinner like everyone else, especially like that tax collector over there! For I never cheat, I don't commit adultery, I go without food twice a week, and I give to God a tenth of everything I earn.' But the corrupt tax collector stood at a distance and dared not even lift his eyes to heaven as he prayed, but beat upon his chest in sorrow, exclaiming, 'God, be merciful to me, a sinner.'

"I tell you, this sinner, not the Pharisee, returned home forgiven! For the proud shall be humbled, but the humble shall be honored."

Then He went southward to the Judean borders and into the area east of the Jordan River. And as always there were the crowds; and as usual He taught them and He healed their sick.

Some Pharisees came to interview Him, and tried to trap Him into saying something that would ruin Him. "Do You permit divorce?" they asked.

"Don't you read the Scriptures?" He replied. "In

Luke 18:7-14; Mark 10:1; Matthew 19:2-4

them it is written that at the beginning God created man and woman, and that a man shall leave his father and mother, and be forever united to his wife. The two shall become one—no longer two, but one! And no man may divorce what God has joined together."

"Then, why," they asked, "did Moses say a man can divorce his wife by merely writing her a letter of dismissal?"

Jesus replied, "Moses did that in recognition of your hard and evil hearts, but it was not what God had originally intended. And no man may separate what God has joined together. And I tell you this, that anyone who divorces his wife, except for fornication, and marries another, commits adultery."

Later, when He was alone with His disciples in the house, they brought up the subject again. He told them, "When a man divorces his wife to marry someone else, he commits adultery against her. And if a wife divorces her husband and remarries, she, too, commits adultery."

Jesus' disciples then said to Him, "If that is how it is, it is better not to marry!"

"Not everyone can accept this statement," Jesus said. "Only those whom God helps. Some are born without the ability to marry, and some are disabled by men, and some refuse to marry for the sake of the Kingdom of Heaven. Let anyone who can, accept My statement."

Once when some mothers were bringing their

Matthew 19:4-8; Mark 10:9; Matthew 19:9; Mark 10:10-12; Matthew 19:10-12; Mark 10:13

children to Jesus to bless them, the disciples shooed them away, telling them not to bother Him. But when Jesus saw what was happening, He was very much displeased with His disciples and said to them, "Let these children come to Me, for the Kingdom of God belongs to such as these. Don't send them away! I tell you seriously that anyone who refuses to come to God as a little child will never be allowed into His Kingdom." And He took the children into His arms and, placing His hands on their heads, He blessed them.

Once a Jewish religious leader asked Him this question: "Good Sir, what shall I do to get to heaven?"

"Do you realize what you are saying when you call me 'good'?" Jesus asked him. "Only God is truly good, and no one else. But to answer your question, you can get to heaven if you keep the commandments!"

"Which ones?" the man asked.

And Jesus replied, "Don't kill, don't commit adultery, don't steal, don't lie, honor your father and mother, and love your neighbor as yourself!"

"I've always obeyed every one of them," the youth replied. "What else must I do?"

Jesus felt genuine love for this man as He looked at him. "You lack only one thing," He told him; "go and sell all you have and give the money to the poor—and you shall have treasure in heaven—and come, follow Me."

Mark 10:13-16; Luke 18:18,19; Matthew 19:17-20; Mark 10:21

Then the man's face fell, and he went sadly away, for he was very rich.

Jesus watched him go, then turned around and said to His disciples, "It's almost impossible for the rich to get into the Kingdom of God!" This amazed them. So Jesus said it again: "Dear children, how hard it is for those who trust in riches to enter the Kingdom of God. It is easier for a camel to go through the eye of a needle than for a rich man to enter the Kingdom of God."

The disciples were incredulous! "Then who in the world can be saved, if not a rich man?" they asked.

Jesus looked at them and said, "Humanly speaking, no one! But with God, everything is possible."

Then Peter began to mention all that he and the other disciples had left behind. "We've given up everything to follow You," he said.

And Jesus replied, "Truly, when I, the Son of Man, shall sit upon My glorious throne in the Kingdom, you My disciples shall sit on twelve thrones judging the twelve tribes of Israel. Let Me assure you that no one has ever given up anything —home, brothers, sisters, mother, father, children, or property—for love of Me and to tell others the Good News, who won't be given back, a hundred times over, homes, brothers, sisters, mothers, children, and land—with persecutions! All these will be his here on earth, and in the world to come he shall have eternal life. But many who seem the most important now shall be the least important then;

Mark 10:22-26; Matthew 19:26; Mark 10:28; Matthew 19:28; Mark 10:29-31 and many who are considered least here shall be greatest there."

"Here is another illustration of the Kingdom of Heaven. The owner of an estate went out early one morning to hire workers for his harvest field. He agreed to pay them $20 a day and sent them off to work. A couple of hours later he was passing a hiring hall and saw some men standing around waiting for jobs, so he sent them also into his fields, telling them he would pay them whatever was right at the end of the day. At noon and again around three o'clock in the afternoon he did the same thing. At five o'clock that evening he was in town again and saw some more men standing around and asked them, 'Why have you been idle all day?' 'Because no one has hired us,' they replied. 'Then go on out and join the others in my fields,' he told them.

"That evening he told the paymaster to call the men in and pay them, beginning with the last men first! When the men hired at five o'clock were paid, each received $20! So when the men hired earlier came to get theirs, they assumed they would receive much more. But they too were paid $20!

"They protested, 'Those fellows worked only one hour, and yet you've paid them just as much as those of us who worked all day in the scorching heat.' 'Friend,' he answered to one, 'I did you no wrong! Didn't you agree to work all day for $20? Take it and go. It is my desire to pay all the same;

Mark 10:31; Matthew 20:1-13

is it against the law to give away my money if I want to? Should you be angry because I am kind?' And so it is that the last shall be first, and the first, last!"

They were on the way to Jerusalem, and Jesus was walking along ahead; and as the disciples were following, they were filled with terror and with dread. Gathering The Twelve around Him, He told them, "As you know, we are going to Jerusalem. And when we get there, all the predictions of the ancient prophets concerning Me will come true. I, the Son of Man, will be arrested and taken before the chief priests and the Jewish leaders, who will sentence Me to die, and hand Me over to the Romans to be killed. They will mock Me and spit on Me and flog Me with their whips and kill Me; and after three days I will come back to life again."

Then James and John, the sons of Zebedee, came over and spoke to Him in a low voice. "Master," they said, "we want You to do us a favor."

"What is it?" He asked.

"We want to sit on the thrones next to Yours in Your kingdom," they said, "one at Your right and the other at Your left!"

But Jesus answered, "You don't know what you are asking! Are you able to drink from the bitter cup of sorrow I must drink from? Or to be baptized with the baptism of suffering I must be baptized with?"

"Oh, yes," they said, "we are!"

Matthew 20:14-16; Mark 10:32; Luke 18:31; Mark 10:33-38

And Jesus said, "You shall indeed drink from My cup and be baptized with My baptism, but I do not have the right to place you next to Me on My throne. Those appointments have already been made."

When the other disciples discovered what James and John had asked, they were very indignant. So Jesus called them to Him and said, "As you know, the kings and great men of the earth lord it over the people; but among you it is different. Whoever wants to be great among you must be your servant! And whoever wants to be greatest of all must be the slave of all. For even I, the Son of Man, am not here to be served, but to help others; and to give My life as a ransom for many."

Mark 10:39-45

Chapter 30

Crowded Schedule

Late in March, A.D. 30

As they left the city of Jericho, a vast crowd followed Him. Now it happened that a blind beggar named Bartimaeus, the son of Timaeus, was sitting beside the road as Jesus was going by. When he heard the noise of a crowd going past, he asked what was happening. He was told that Jesus from Nazareth was going by, so he began shouting, "Jesus, Son of David, have mercy on me!"

"Shut up!" some of the people yelled at him.

But he only shouted the louder, again and again, "O, Son of David, have mercy on me!"

Jesus stopped in the road when He heard him and said, "Tell him to come here."

So they called the blind man. "You lucky fellow," they said, "come on, He is calling you!"

Bartimaeus yanked off his old coat and flung it aside, jumped up and came to Jesus.

"What do you want Me to do for you?" Jesus asked.

"O Teacher," the blind man said, "I want to see!"

And Jesus said, "All right, begin seeing! Your faith has healed you!" And instantly the man could

Matthew 20:29; Mark 10:46; Luke 18:36-38; Mark 10:48-51; Luke 18:42,43

see, and followed Jesus, praising God. And all who saw it happen praised God too.

As Jesus was passing through Jericho, a man named Zacchaeus, one of the most influential Jews in the Roman tax-collecting business and of course a very rich man, tried to get a look at Jesus, but he was too short to see over the crowds. So he ran ahead and climbed into a sycamore tree beside the road to see Him, and watched from there.

When Jesus came by He looked up at Zacchaeus and called him by name! "Zacchaeus," He said, "Quick! Come down! For I am going to be guest in your home today!" Zacchaeus climbed down hurriedly and took Jesus to his house in great excitement and joy.

But the crowds were displeased. "He has gone to be the guest of a notorious sinner," they grumbled.

Meanwhile Zacchaeus stood before the Lord and said, "Sir, from now on I will give half my wealth to the poor, and if I find I have overcharged anyone on his taxes, I will penalize myself by giving him back four times as much!"

Jesus told him, "This shows that salvation has come to this home today. This man was one of the lost sons of Abraham, and I, the Son of Man, have come to search for and save such souls as his."

And because Jesus was nearing Jerusalem, He told a story to correct the impression that the Kingdom of God would begin right away.

"A nobleman living in a certain province was

Luke 18:43; Luke 19:1-12

called away to the distant capital of the empire to be crowned king of his province. Before he left he called together ten assistants, his slaves, and gave them each $2,000 to invest while he was gone. But some of his people hated him and sent him their declaration of independence, stating that they had rebelled and would not acknowledge him as their king.

"Upon his return he called in the men to whom he had given the money, to find out what they had done with it, and what their profits were. The first man reported a tremendous gain—ten times as much as the original amount! 'Fine!' the king exclaimed. 'You are a good man. You have been faithful with the little I entrusted to you, and as your reward, you shall be governor of ten cities.'

"The next man came with his report of a large gain—five times the original amount. 'All right!' his master said. 'You can be governor over five cities.' But another brought back only the money with which he had started. 'I've kept it safe,' he said, 'because I was afraid you would demand my profits, for you are a hard man to deal with, taking what isn't yours and even confiscating the crops that others plant!'

" 'You vile and wicked slave,' the king roared. 'Hard, am I? That's exactly how I'll be toward you! If you knew so much about me and how tough I am, then why didn't you deposit the money in the

Luke 19:12-23

bank so that at least I could get some interest on it?'

"Then turning to the others standing by he ordered, 'Take the money away from him and give it to the man who earned the most.'

" 'But, sir,' they said, 'he has enough already!'

" 'Yes,' the king replied, 'but it is always true that those who have, get more, and those who have little, soon lose even that. And now about these enemies of mine who revolted—bring them in and execute them before me.' "

After telling this story, Jesus went on towards Jerusalem, walking along ahead of His disciples.

The Passover, a Jewish holy day, was near, and many country people arrived in Jerusalem several days early so that they could go through the cleansing ceremony before the Passover began. They wanted to see Jesus, and as they gossiped in the Temple, they asked each other, "What do you think? Will He come for the Passover?"

Meanwhile the chief priests and Pharisees had publicly announced that anyone seeing Jesus must report Him immediately so that they could arrest Him.

Saturday, April 1, A.D. 30

Six days before the Passover ceremonies began, Jesus arrived in Bethany where Lazarus was—the man He had brought back to life. A banquet was

Luke 19:23-28; John 11:55-57; John 12:1,2

prepared in Jesus' honor at the home of Simon the leper. Martha served, and Lazarus sat at the table with Him.

Then Mary took a jar of costly perfume made from essence of nard, and anointed Jesus' feet with it and wiped them with her hair. And the house was filled with fragrance. But Judas Iscariot, one of His disciples—the one who would betray Him—said, "That perfume was worth a fortune! It should have been sold for $6,000 and the money given to the poor!" Not that he cared for the poor, but he was in charge of the disciples' funds and often dipped into them for his own use!

Jesus replied, "Let her alone. She did it in preparation for My burial. You can always help the poor, but I won't be with you very long! She has done what she could, and has anointed My body ahead of time for burial. And I tell you this in solemn truth, that wherever the Good News is preached throughout the world, this woman's deed will be remembered and praised."

When the ordinary people of Jerusalem heard of His arrival, they flocked to see Him and also to see Lazarus—the man who had come back to life again. Then the chief priests decided to kill Lazarus too, for it was because of him that many of the Jewish leaders had deserted and believed in Jesus as their Messiah.

John 12:2; Mark 14:3; John 12:3-5; Mark 14:5; John 12:6-8; Mark 14:8,9; John 12:9-11

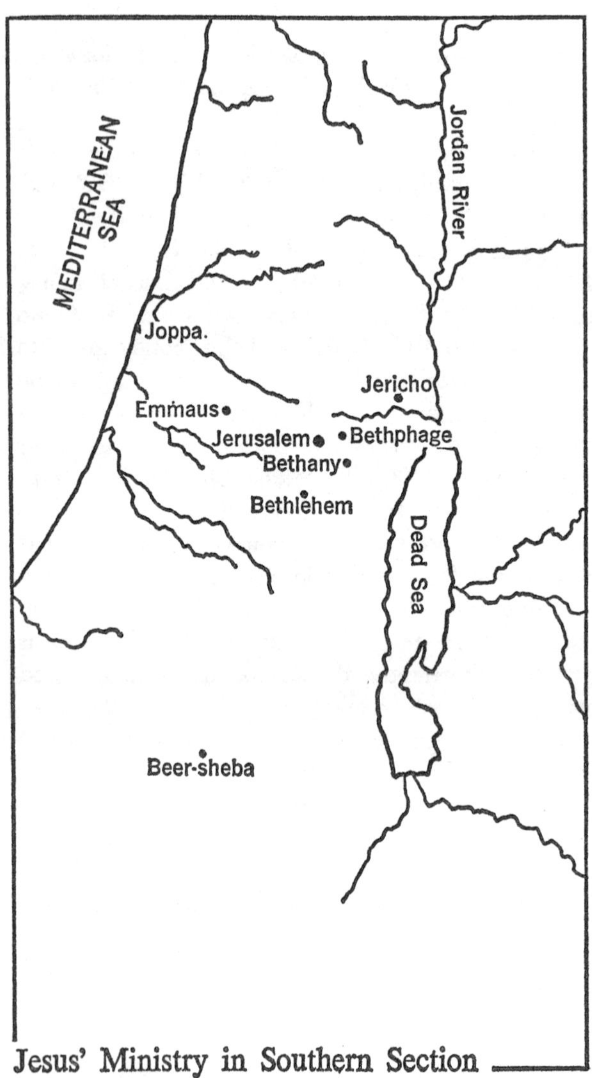

Jesus' Ministry in Southern Section

Don't be upset.

Trust God—and trust me.

PART 4

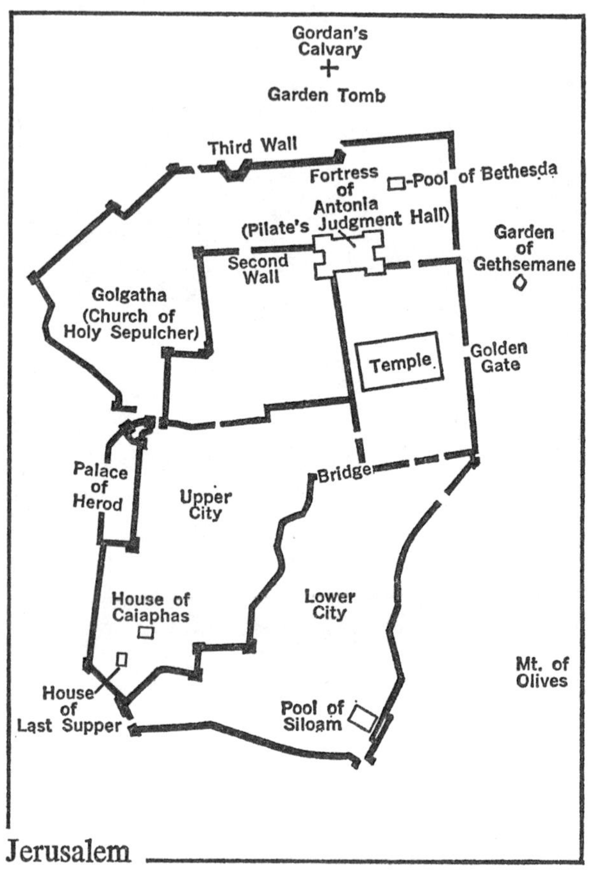
Gordan's Calvary
Garden Tomb
Third Wall
Fortress of Antonia (Pilate's Judgment Hall)
Pool of Bethesda
Garden of Gethsemane
Second Wall
Golgatha (Church of Holy Sepulcher)
Temple
Golden Gate
Palace of Herod
Upper City
Bridge
House of Caiaphas
Lower City
Mt. of Olives
House of Last Supper
Pool of Siloam
Jerusalem

Chapter 31

Acclaimed and Challenged

Sunday, April 2, A.D. 30

The next day, as Jesus and the disciples approached Jerusalem, near the village of Bethphage on the Mount of Olives, Jesus sent two of them into the village ahead. "Go into that village over there," He told them, "and just as you enter you will see a colt tied up that has never been ridden. Untie him and bring him here. And if anyone asks you what you are doing, just say, 'Our Master needs him and will return him soon.'" This was done to fulfill the ancient prophecy, "Tell Jerusalem her King is coming to her, riding humbly on a donkey's colt!"

The two disciples did as Jesus said, and sure enough, as they were untying it, the owners demanded an explanation. "What are you doing?" they asked. "Why are you untying our colt?"

And the disciples simply replied, "The Lord needs him!" So they brought the colt to Jesus and threw some of their clothing across its back for Jesus to sit on. Then the crowds spread out their robes along the road ahead of Him, and as they reached the place where the road started down from the Mount of Olives, the whole procession began to shout and sing as they walked along,

John 12:12; Matthew 21:1; Mark 11:2,3; Matthew 21:4-6; Luke 19:33-37

praising God for all the wonderful miracles Jesus had done. "God has given us a King!" they exulted. "Long live the King! Let all heaven rejoice! Glory to God in the highest heavens!" The news that Jesus was on the way to Jerusalem swept through the city, and a huge crowd of Passover visitors took palm branches and went down the road to meet Him, shouting, "The Savior! God bless the King of Israel! Hail to God's Ambassador!"

But some of the Pharisees among the crowd said, "Sir, rebuke Your followers for saying things like that!"

He replied, "If they kept quiet, the stones along the road would burst into cheers!"

But then as they came closer to Jerusalem and He saw the city ahead, He began to cry. "Eternal peace was within your reach and you have turned it down," He wept, "and now it is too late. Your enemies will pile up earth against your walls and encircle you and close in on you, and crush you to the ground, and your children within you; your enemies will not leave one stone upon another—for you have rejected the opportunity God offered you."

At the time, His disciples didn't realize that this was a fulfillment of prophecy; but after Jesus returned to His glory in heaven, they noticed how many prophecies of Scripture had come true before their eyes.

And those in the crowd who had seen Jesus call

Luke 19:37,38; John 12:12,13; Luke 19:39-44; John 12:16,17

Lazarus back to life were telling all about it. In fact that was why so many went out to meet Him—because they had heard about this mighty miracle. Then the Pharisees said to each other, "We've lost. Look—the whole world has gone after Him!"

And so He entered Jerusalem, and went into the Temple. He looked carefully at everything around Him and then left—for now it was late in the afternoon—and went out to Bethany with the twelve disciples.

Monday, April 3, A.D. 30

The next morning as they left Bethany, He felt hungry. A little way off He noticed a fig tree in full leaf. So He went over to see if He could find any figs on it. But no, there were only leaves, for it was too early in the season for fruit. Then Jesus said to the tree, "You shall never bear fruit again!" And the disciples heard Him say it.

When they arrived back in Jerusalem, He went to the Temple and began to drive out the merchants and their customers, and knocked over the tables of the moneychangers, and the stalls of those selling doves, and stopped everyone from bringing in loads of merchandise. He told them, "It is written in the Scriptures, 'My Temple is to be a place of prayer for all nations,' but you have turned it into a den of robbers."

And now the blind and crippled came to Him in

John 12:17-19; Mark 11:11-17; Matthew 21:14

the Temple, and He healed them there. But when the chief priests and other Jewish leaders saw these wonderful miracles, and heard even the little children in the Temple shouting, "God bless the Son of David," They were disturbed and indignant and said to Him, "Do you hear what these children are saying?"

"Yes," Jesus told them. "Didn't you ever read the Scriptures? For they say, 'Even little babies shall praise Him!' "

After that He taught daily in the Temple, but the chief priests and other religious leaders and the business community were trying to find some way to get rid of Him. But they could think of nothing, for He was a hero to the people—they hung on every word He said.

That evening as usual they left the city.

Tuesday, April 4, A.D. 30

Next morning, as the disciples passed the fig tree He had cursed, they saw that it was withered from the roots! Then Peter remembered what Jesus had said to the tree on the previous day, and exclaimed, "Look, Teacher! The fig tree You cursed has withered!"

In reply Jesus said to the disciples, "If you only have faith in God—this is the absolute truth—you can say to this Mount of Olives, 'Rise up and fall into the Mediterranean,' and your command will be

Matthew 21:14-16; Luke 19:47,48; Mark 11:19-23

obeyed. All that's required is that you really believe and have no doubt! Listen to Me! You can pray for anything, and if you believe you have it, it's yours! But when you are praying, forgive anyone you are holding a grudge against, so that your Father in heaven may forgive you your sins."

When He had returned to the Temple and was teaching, the chief priests and other Jewish leaders came up to Him and demanded to know by whose authority He had thrown the merchants out the day before.

"I'll tell you if you answer one question first," Jesus replied. "Was John the Baptist sent from God, or not?"

They talked it over among themselves. "If we say, 'From God,' then He will ask why we didn't believe John. And if we deny that God sent him, we'll be mobbed, for this crowd all think he was a prophet." So they finally replied, "We don't know!"

And Jesus said, "Then I won't answer your question either!

"But what do you think about this? A man with two sons told the older boy, 'Son, go out and work on the farm today.' 'I won't,' he answered, but later he changed his mind and went! Then the father told the youngest, 'You go!' and he said, 'Yes, sir, I will!' But he didn't!

"Which of the two was obeying his father?"

They replied, "The first, of course."

Then Jesus explained His meaning: "Surely evil

Mark 11:23-25; Matthew 21:23-31

men and prostitutes will get into the Kingdom before you do. For John the Baptist told you to repent and turn to God, and you wouldn't, while very evil men and prostitutes did! And even when you saw this happening, you refused to repent so that you could believe.

"Now listen to this story: A certain landowner planted a vineyard with a hedge around it, and built a platform for the watchman, then leased the vineyard to some farmers on a sharecrop basis, and went away to live in another country. At the time of the grape harvest, he sent his agents to the farmers to collect his share. But the farmers attacked his men, beat one, killed one and stoned another. Then he sent a larger group of his men to collect for him, but the results were the same.

"Finally the owner sent his son, thinking they would surely respect him. But when these farmers saw the son coming they said among themselves, 'He is the heir to this estate; come on, let's kill him, and get it for ourselves!' So they dragged him out of the vineyard and killed him.

"When the owner returns, what do you think he will do to those farmers?"

The Jewish leaders replied, "He will put the wicked men to a horrible death, and lease the vineyard to others who will pay him promptly."

Then Jesus asked them, "Didn't you ever read in the Scriptures, 'The stone rejected by the builders has been made the honored cornerstone? How re-

Matthew 21:31-42

markable! What an amazing thing the Lord has done.' What I mean is that the Kingdom of God shall be taken away from you, and given to a nation that will give God His share of the crop. All who stumble on this rock of truth shall be broken, but those it falls on will be scattered as dust."

The Jewish leaders wanted to arrest Him then and there for using this illustration, for they knew He was pointing at them—they were the wicked farmers in His story. But they were afraid to touch Him for fear of a mob. So they left Him and went away.

Jesus told several other stories to show what the Kingdom of Heaven is like. "For instance," He said, "it can be illustrated by the story of a king who prepared a great wedding dinner for his son. Many guests were invited, and when the banquet was ready, he sent messengers to notify everyone that it was time to come. But they all refused! So he sent other servants to tell them, 'Everything is ready and the roast is in the oven. Hurry!' But the guests he had invited merely laughed and went on about their business, one to his farm, another to his store; others beat up his messengers and treated them shamefully, even killing some of them. The angry king sent out his army and destroyed the murderers and burned their city.

"Then he said to his servants, 'The wedding feast is ready, and the guests I invited weren't worthy of

Matthew 21:42-44; Mark 12:12; Matthew 22:1-8

the honor. Now go out to the street corners and invite everyone you see.'

"So the servants did, and brought in all they could find, good and bad alike; and the banquet hall was filled with guests. But when the king came in to meet the guests, he noticed a man who wasn't wearing the wedding robe provided for him. 'Friend,' he asked, 'how does it happen that you are here without a wedding robe?' And the man had no reply. Then the king said to his aides, 'Bind him hand and foot and throw him out into the outer darkness where there is weeping and gnashing of teeth.'

"For many are called, but few are chosen."

Matthew 22:8-14

Chapter 32

Trick Questions

Then the Pharisees called a meeting to think of some way to trap Him into saying something for which they could arrest Him. They decided to send some of their men along with the Herodians to ask Him this question: "Sir, we know You are very honest and teach the truth regardless of the consequences, without fear or favor. Now tell us, is it right to pay taxes to the Roman government or not?"

But Jesus saw what they were after. "You hypocrites!" He said. "Who are you trying to fool with your trick questions? Here, show Me a coin." And they handed Him a penny.

"Whose picture is on it?" He asked them. "And whose name is this beneath the picture?"

"Caesar's," they replied.

"Well then," He said, "give it to Caesar if it is his, and give God everything that belongs to God." His reply surprised and baffled them and they went away.

But that same day some of the Sadducees, who say there is no resurrection after death, came to Him and asked, "Sir, Moses said that if a man died without children, his brother should marry the widow and their children would get all the dead

Matthew 22:15-24

man's property. Well, we had among us a family of seven brothers. The first of these men married and then died, without children, so his widow became the second brother's wife. This brother also died without children, and the wife was passed to the next brother, and so on until she had been the wife of each of them. And then she also died. So whose wife will she be in the resurrection? For she was the wife of all seven of them!"

But Jesus said, "Your error is caused by your ignorance of the Scriptures and God's power! For in the resurrection there is no marriage; everyone is as the angels in heaven. But now as to whether there will be a resurrection! Have you never read in the book of Exodus about Moses and the burning bush? God said to Moses, 'I am the God of Abraham, and I am the God of Isaac, and I am the God of Jacob.' God was telling Moses that these men, though dead for hundreds of years, were still very much alive, for He would not have said, 'I *am* the God' of those who didn't exist! You have made a serious error."

The crowds were profoundly impressed by His answers—but not the Pharisees! When they heard He had routed the Sadducees with His reply, they thought up a fresh question of their own to ask Him. One of them, a lawyer, spoke up, "Sir, which is the most important command in the laws of Moses?"

Jesus replied, "'Love the Lord your God with all your heart, soul and mind.' This is the great first

Matthew 22:24-30; Mark 12:26,27; Matthew 22:33-38

commandment. The second in importance is similar, 'Love your neighbor as much as you love yourself.' All the other commandments and all the demands of the prophets stem from these two laws, and are fulfilled in them. Keep them and you are obeying all the others."

The teacher of religion replied, "Sir, You have spoken a true word in saying that there is only one God and no other. And I know it is far more important to love Him with all my heart and understanding and strength, and to love others as myself, than to offer all kinds of sacrifices on the altar of the Temple."

Realizing this man's understanding, Jesus said to him, "You are not far from the Kingdom of God."

While the Pharisees surrounded Him, He asked them a question: "What about the Messiah? Whose son is He?"

"The son of David," they replied.

"Then why does David, speaking under inspiration of the Holy Spirit, call Him 'Lord'?" Jesus asked them. "For David said, 'The Lord said to My Lord, Sit at My right hand until I put Your enemies beneath Your feet.' Since David called Him 'Lord,' how can He merely be his son?"

They had no answer. And after that no one dared ask Him any more questions.

Then Jesus said to the crowds, and to His disciples, "You would think these Jewish leaders and these Pharisees were Moses, the way they keep

Matthew 22:38-40; Mark 12:32-34; Matthew 22:41-46; Matthew 23:1

making up so many laws! And of course you should obey their every whim! It may be all right to do what they say, but above anything else, don't follow their example! For they don't do what they tell you to do! They load you with impossible demands that they themselves don't even try to keep. All they do is done for show. For they love to wear the robes of the rich and scholarly, and to have everyone bow to them as they walk through the markets. They act holy by wearing on their arms large prayer boxes with Scripture verses inside, and by lengthening the memorial fringes of their robes! And how they love to sit at the head table at banquets, and in the reserved pews in the synagogue! But they shamelessly cheat widows out of their homes and then, to cover up the kind of men they really are, they pretend to be pious by praying long prayers in public! Because of this, their punishment will be the greater.

"How they enjoy the deference paid them on the streets, and to be called 'Rabbi' and 'Master'! Don't ever let anyone call you that! For only God is your Rabbi and all of you are on the same level, as brothers. And don't address anyone here on earth as 'Father,' for only God in heaven should be addressed like that. And don't be called 'Master,' for only one is your master, even the Messiah.

"The more lowly your service to others, the greater you are. To be the greatest, be a servant. But those who think themselves great shall be

Matthew 23:1-5; Mark 12:38; Matthew 23:5,6; Mark 12:40; Matthew 23:7-12 disappointed and humbled; and those who humble themselves shall be exalted.

"Woe to you, Pharisees, and you other religious leaders! Hypocrites! For you won't let others enter the Kingdom of Heaven, and won't go in yourselves. And you pretend to be holy, with all your long, public prayers in the streets, while you are evicting widows from their homes! Hypocrites! Yes, woe upon you, hypocrites! For you go to all lengths to make one convert, and then turn him into twice the son of hell you are yourselves.

"Blind guides! Woe upon you! For your rule is that to swear 'By God's Temple' means nothing—you can break that oath; but to swear 'By the gold in the Temple' is binding! Blind fools! Which is greater, the gold, or the Temple that sanctifies the gold?

"And you say that to take an oath 'By the altar' can be broken, but to swear 'By the gifts on the altar' is binding! Blind! For which is greater, the gift on the altar, or the altar itself that sanctifies the gift? When you swear 'By the altar' you are swearing by it and everything on it, and when you swear 'By the Temple' you are swearing by it, and by God who lives in it. And when you swear 'By heavens' you are swearing by the Throne of God and by God Himself.

"Yes, woe upon you, Pharisees, and you other religious leaders—hypocrites! For you tithe down to the last mint leaf in your garden, but ignore the

Matthew 23:12-23

important things—justice and mercy and faith. Yes, you should tithe, but you shouldn't leave the more important things undone. Blind guides! You strain out a gnat and swallow a camel!

"Woe to you, Pharisees, and you religious leaders —hypocrites! You are so careful to polish the outside of the cup, but the inside is foul with extortion and greed. Blind Pharisees! First cleanse the inside of the cup, and then the whole cup will be clean.

"Woe to you, Pharisees, and you religious leaders! You are like beautiful sepulchers—full of dead men's bones, and of foulness and corruption. You try to look like saintly men, but underneath those pious robes are hearts besmirched with every sort of hypocrisy and sin.

"Yes, woe to you, Pharisees, and you religious leaders—hypocrites! For you build monuments to the prophets killed by your fathers and lay flowers on the graves of the godly men they destroyed, and say, 'We certainly would never have acted like our fathers did.' In saying that, you are accusing yourselves of being the sons of wicked men. And you follow in their steps, filling up the full measure of evil. Snakes! Sons of vipers! How shall you escape the judgment of hell?

"I will send you prophets and spirit-filled men, and inspired writers, and you will kill some by crucifixion, and rip open the backs of others with whips in your synagogues, and hound them from city to city, so that you will become guilty of all the

Matthew 23:23-35

blood of murdered godly men from righteous Abel to Zechariah (son of Barachiah), slain by you in the Temple between the altar and the sanctuary. Yes, all the accumulated judgment of the centuries shall break upon the heads of this very generation.

"O Jerusalem, Jerusalem, the city that kills the prophets, and stones all those God sends to her! How often I have wanted to gather your children together as a hen gathers her chicks beneath her wings, and you wouldn't let Me. And now your house is left to you, desolate. For I tell you this, you will never see Me again until you are ready to welcome the One sent to you from God."

Matthew 23:35-39

Chapter 33

Disturbing Words

As He stood in the Temple, He was watching the rich men tossing their gifts into the collection box. Then a poor widow came and dropped in two small copper coins.

He called His disciples to Him. "Really," He remarked, "this poor widow has given more than all the rest of them combined. For they have given a little of what they didn't need, but she, poor as she is, has given everything she has."

Some Greeks who had come to Jerusalem to attend the Passover paid a visit to Philip, who was from Bethsaida, and said, "Sir, we want to meet Jesus." Philip told Andrew about it, and they went together to ask Jesus.

Jesus replied that the time had come for Him to return to His glory in heaven, and that "I must fall and die like a kernel of wheat that falls between the furrows of the earth. Unless I die, I will be alone—a single seed. But My death will produce many new wheat kernels—a plentiful harvest of new lives.

"If you love your life down here—you will lose it! If you despise your life down here—you will exchange it for eternal glory! If these Greeks want to be My disciples, tell them to come and follow Me,

Luke 21:1,2; Mark 12:43; Luke 21:3,4; John 12:20-26

for My servants must be where I am. And if they follow Me, the Father will honor them.

"Now My soul is deeply troubled. Shall I pray, 'Father, save Me from what lies ahead'? But that is the very reason why I came! Father, bring glory and honor to Your name."

Then a voice spoke from heaven saying, "I have already done this, and I will do it again."

When the crowd heard the voice, some of them thought it was thunder, while others declared an angel had spoken to Him.

Then Jesus told them, "The voice was for your benefit, not Mine. The time of judgment for the world has come—and the time when Satan, the prince of this world, shall be cast out. And when I am lifted up on the cross, I will draw everyone to Me."

He said this to indicate how He was going to die.

"Die?" asked the crowd. "We understood that the Messiah would live forever and never die. Why are You saying He will die? What Messiah are You talking about?"

Jesus replied, "My light will shine out for you just a little while longer. Walk in it while you can, and go where you want to go before the darkness falls, for then it will be too late for you to find your way. Make use of the Light while there is still time; then you will become sons of Light." After saying these things, Jesus went away and was hidden from them.

John 12:26-36

But despite all the miracles He had done, most of the people would not believe He was the Messiah. This is exactly what Isaiah the prophet had predicted: "Lord, who will believe us? Who will accept God's mighty miracles as proof?" But they couldn't believe, for as Isaiah also said: "God has blinded their eyes and hardened their hearts so that they can neither see nor understand nor turn to Me to heal them." Isaiah was referring to Jesus when he made this prediction, for he had seen a vision of the Messiah's glory.

However, even many of the Jewish leaders believed Him to be the Messiah but wouldn't admit it to anyone because of their fear that the Pharisees would excommunicate them from the synagogue, for they loved the praise of men more than the praise of God.

Jesus shouted to the crowds, "If you trust Me, you are really trusting God. For when you see Me, you are seeing the one who sent Me.

"I have come as a Light to shine in this dark world, so that all who put their trust in Me will no longer wander in the darkness. If anyone hears Me and doesn't obey Me, I am not his judge—for I have come to save the world and not to judge it. But all who reject Me and My message will be judged at the Day of Judgment by the truths I have spoken. For these are not My own ideas, but I have told you what the Father said to tell you, and I

John 12:37-50

know His instructions give eternal life; so whatever He tells Me to say, I say!"

As He was leaving the Temple, one of His disciples said, "Teacher, what beautiful buildings these are! Look at the decorated stonework on the walls!"

Jesus replied, "Yes, look while you have the chance! For not one stone will be left upon another, except as ruins!" And as He sat on the slopes of the Mount of Olives across the valley from Jerusalem, Peter, James, John, and Andrew got alone with Him and asked Him, "Just when is all this going to happen to the Temple? Will there be some warning ahead of time?"

He replied, "Don't let anyone mislead you. For many will come announcing themselves as the Messiah, and saying, 'The time has come.' Don't believe them! And when you hear of wars and insurrections beginning, don't panic. True, wars must come, but the end won't follow immediately—for nation shall rise against nation and kingdom against kingdom, and there will be great earthquakes, and famines in many lands, and epidemics, and terrifying things happening in the heavens. These herald only the early stages of the anguish ahead.

"But when these things begin to happen, watch out! For you will be in great danger. You will be dragged before the courts, and beaten in the synagogues, and accused before governors and kings of being My followers. This is your opportunity to tell them the Good News. But when you are arrested

John 12:50; Mark 13:1-4; Luke 21:8-11; Mark 13:8,9,11

and stand trial, don't worry about what to say in your defense. Just say what God tells you to! Then you will not be speaking, but the Holy Spirit!

"Brothers will betray each other to death; fathers will betray their own children, and children will betray their parents to be killed. And everyone will hate you because you are Mine and are called by My name. But not a hair of your head will perish! For if you stand firm, you will win your souls.

"And many shall fall back and betray one another, and hate each other. And many false prophets will appear, and lead many astray. Sin will be rampant everywhere and will cool the love of many. But those enduring to the end will be saved. And the Good News about the Kingdom will be preached in the whole world, so that all nations will hear it, and then, finally, the end will come.

"So when you see the horrible thing told about by Daniel the prophet standing in a holy place (Note to the reader: You know what is meant!) then those in Judea must flee into the Judean hills; those on their porches must not even go inside to pack before they flee. Those in the fields should not return to their homes for their clothes. For those will be days of God's judgment, and the words of the ancient Scriptures written by the prophets will be abundantly fulfilled.

"Woe to expectant mothers in those days, and those with tiny babies. For there will be great distress upon this nation and wrath upon this peo-

Mark 13:11,12; Luke 21:17-19; Matthew 24:10-18; Luke 21:22,23

ple. They will be brutally killed by enemy weapons, or sent away as exiles and captives to all the nations of the world; and Jerusalem shall be conquered and trampled down by the Gentiles until the period of Gentile triumph ends in God's good time.

"And pray that your flight will not be in winter, or on the Sabbath. For there will be persecution such as the world has never before seen in all its history, and will never see again. In fact, unless those days are shortened, all mankind will perish. But they will be shortened for the sake of God's chosen people.

"Then if anyone tells you, 'The Messiah has arrived at such and such a place, or has appeared here or there or in the village yonder,' don't believe it. For false Christs shall arise, and false prophets, and will do wonderful miracles, so that if it were possible, even God's chosen ones would be deceived.

"See, I have warned you. So if someone tells you the Messiah has returned and is out in the desert, don't bother to go and look. Or, that He is hiding at a certain place, don't believe it! For as the lightning flashes across the sky from east to west, so shall My coming be, when I, the Son of all Man, return. And wherever the carcass is, there the vultures will gather.

"Immediately after the persecution of those days, the sun will be darkened, and the moon turn black, and the stars will seem to fall from the heavens, and the evil powers overshadowing the earth will

Luke 21:24; Matthew 24:20-29

be convulsed. And then at last there will appear a signal in the heavens of My coming; and there will be deep mourning all around the earth. Then there will be strange events in the skies—warnings, evil omens and portents in the sun, moon and stars; and down here on earth the nations will be in turmoil, perplexed by the roaring seas and strange tides. The courage of many people will falter because of the fearful fate they see coming upon the earth, for the stability of the very heavens will be broken up.

"And the nations of the world will see Me arrive in the clouds of heaven, with power and great glory. And I shall send forth My angels with the sound of a mighty trumpet blast, and they will gather My chosen ones from the farthest ends of the earth and heaven. So when all these things begin to happen, stand straight and look up! For your salvation is near."

Matthew 24:29,30; Luke 21:25,26; Matthew 24:30,31; Luke 21:28

Chapter 34

A Look into the Future

"Now learn a lesson from the fig tree! When her branch is tender and the leaves begin to sprout, you know that summer is almost here. Just so, when you see all these things beginning to happen, you can know that My return is near, even at the doors! Truly, only then will this age come to its close. Heaven and earth will disappear, but My words remain forever.

"But no one knows the date and hour when the end will be—not even the angels. No, nor even God's Son. Only the Father knows. The world will be at ease—banquets and parties and weddings—just as it was in Noah's time before the sudden coming of the flood, when they wouldn't believe what was going to happen until the flood came and took them all away. So shall My coming be. Then two men will be working together in the fields, and one will be taken, the other left. Two women will be going about their household tasks; one will be taken, the other left. So be prepared for you don't know what day your Lord is coming.

"My coming can be compared with that of a man going on a trip to another country. He lays out his employees' work for them to do while he is gone, and tells the gatekeeper to watch for his arrival.

Matthew 24:32-42; Mark 13:34

Keep a sharp lookout! For you do not know when I will come, at evening, at midnight, early dawn or late daybreak. Don't let Me arrive unexpectedly and find you dozing. I say this to you and to everyone else: Watch! Just as a man can prevent trouble from thieves by keeping watch for them, so also you can avoid trouble by being always ready for My unannounced return.

"Are you a wise and faithful servant of the Lord? Have I given you the task of managing My household, to feed My children day by day? Blessings on you, if I return and find you faithfully doing your work. I will put such faithful ones in charge of everything I own! But if you are evil and say to yourself, 'My Lord won't be coming soon,' and begin oppressing your fellow servants, partying and getting drunk, your Lord will arrive unannounced and unexpected, and severely whip you and send you off to the judgment of the hypocrites; there shall be weeping and gnashing of teeth.

"The Kingdom of Heaven can be illustrated by the story of ten bridesmaids, who took their lamps and went to meet the bridegroom. But only five of them were wise enough to fill their lamps with oil, while the other five were foolish and forgot. So, when the bridegroom was delayed, they lay down to rest until midnight, when they were roused by the cry, 'The bridegroom is coming! Come out and welcome him!' Promptly all the girls jumped up and trimmed their lamps.

Mark 13:35-37; Matthew 24:43-51; Matthew 25:1-7

"Then the five who hadn't any oil begged the others to share with them, for their lamps were going out. But the others replied, 'We haven't enough! Go instead to the shops and buy some for yourselves.' But while they were gone, the bridegroom came, and those who were ready went in with him to the marriage feast, and the door was locked. Later, when the other five returned, they stood outside, calling, 'Sir, open the door for us!' But he called back, 'Go away! It is too late!'

"So stay awake and be prepared, for you do not know the date or moment of My return.

"Again, the Kingdom of Heaven can be illustrated by the story of a man going into another country, who called together his servants and loaned them money to invest for him while he was gone. He gave $5,000 to one, $2,000 to another, and $1,000 to the last–dividing it in proportion to their ability–and then left on his trip. The man who received $5,000 began immediately to buy and sell with it and soon earned another $5,000. The man with $2,000 went right to work too, and earned another $2,000. But the man getting $1,000 dug a hole in the ground and hid the money for safekeeping!

"After a long time their master returned from his trip and called them to him to give account of his money. The man to whom he had entrusted $5,000 brought him $10,000! His master praised him for good work. 'You have been faithful in handling this small amount,' he told him, 'so now I will give you many more responsibilities. Begin the joyous tasks I have assigned to you!'

"Next came the man who had received the $2,000, with the report, 'Sir, you gave me $2,000 to use, and I have doubled it!' 'Good work,' his master said, 'You are a good and faithful servant. You have been faithful over this small amount, so now I will give you much more.'

"Then the man with the $1,000 came and said, 'Sir, I knew you were a hard man and I was afraid you would rob me of what I earned, so I hid your money in the earth and here it is!' But his master replied, 'Wicked man! Lazy slave! Since you knew I would want your profit, you should at least have put my money in the bank so I would get the interest! Take the money from this man and give it to the man with the $10,000!

" 'For the man who uses well what he is given shall be given more, and he shall have abundance. But from the man who is unfaithful, even what little responsibility he has shall be taken from him. And throw the useless servant out into outer darkness: there shall be weeping and gnashing of teeth.'

"But when I, the Son of Man, shall come in My glory, and all the angels with Me, then I shall sit upon My throne of glory. And all the nations shall be gathered before Me. And I will separate them as a shepherd separates the sheep from the goats, and

Matthew 25:21-32

place the sheep at My right hand, and the goats at My left.

"Then I, the King, shall say to those at My right, 'Come, blessed of My Father, into the Kingdom prepared for you from the founding of the world. For I was hungry and you fed Me; I was thirsty and you gave Me water; I was a stranger and you invited Me into your homes; naked, and you clothed Me; sick, and in prison, and you visited Me.'

"Then these righteous ones will reply, 'Sir, when did we ever see You hungry and feed You? Or thirsty and give You anything to drink? Or a stranger, and helped You? Or naked, and clothed You? When did we ever see You sick or in prison, and visit You? And I, the King, shall tell them, 'When you did it to these My brothers you were doing it to Me!'

"Then I shall turn to those on My left and say, 'Away with you, you cursed ones, into the eternal fire prepared for the devil and his demons. For I was hungry and you wouldn't feed Me; thirsty, and you wouldn't give Me anything to drink; a stranger, and you refused Me hospitality; naked, and you wouldn't clothe Me; sick, and in prison, and you didn't visit Me.'

"Then they will reply, 'Lord, when did we ever see You hungry or thirsty or a stranger, or naked, or sick, or in prison, and not help You?' And I shall answer, 'When you refused to help the least of

Matthew 25:33-45

these My brothers, you were refusing help to Me.' And they will go away into eternal punishment; but the righteous into everlasting life."

And now the Passover celebration was drawing near—the Jewish festival when only bread made without yeast was used. When Jesus had finished saying all these things, He told His disciples, "As you know, the Passover celebration begins in two days and I shall be betrayed and crucified."

At that very moment, the chief priests and other Jewish officials were meeting at the residence of Caiaphas, the High Priest, to discuss ways of capturing Jesus quietly, and killing Him. "But not during the Passover celebration," they agreed, "for there would be a riot."

When Satan entered into Judas Iscariot, one of the twelve disciples, he went over to the chief priests and captains of the Temple guards and asked, "How much will you pay me to get Jesus into your hands?" And they gave him thirty silver coins. From that time on, Judas watched for an opportunity to betray Jesus to them when the crowds weren't around.

Matthew 25:45,46; Luke 22:1; Matthew 26:1-5; Luke 22:3,4; Matthew 26:15,16; Luke 22:6

Chapter 35

Unforgettable Meal

Thursday evening, April 6, A.D. 30

Now the day of the Passover celebration arrived when the Passover lamb was killed and eaten with the unleavened bread. Jesus sent Peter and John ahead to find a place to prepare their Passover meal.

"Where do You want us to go?" they asked.

And He replied, "As soon as you enter Jerusalem, you will see a man walking along carrying a pitcher of water. Follow him into the house he enters, and say to the man who lives there, 'Our Teacher says for you to show us the guest room where He can eat the Passover meal with His disciples.' He will take you upstairs to a large room all ready for us. That is the place. Go ahead and prepare the meal there."

They went off to the city and found everything just as Jesus had said. And they prepared the Passover supper. Jesus and the others arrived, and at the proper time all sat down together at the table, and He said, "I have looked forward to this hour with deep longing, anxious to eat this Passover meal with you before My suffering begins. For I tell you now that I won't eat it again until all it

Luke 22:7-16

represents has taken place in the Kingdom of God."

As they were eating, Jesus took a small loaf of bread and blessed it and broke it apart and gave it to the disciples and said, "Take it and eat it, for this is My body!"

And He took a cup of wine and gave thanks for it and gave it to them and said, "Each one drink from it, for this is My blood, sealing the new covenant. It is poured out to forgive the sins of multitudes. Mark My words—I will not drink this wine again until the day I drink it new with you in My Father's kingdom."

And they began to argue among themselves as to who would have the highest rank in the coming Kingdom. Jesus told them, "In this world the kings and great men order about the slaves, who have no choice but to like it! But among you, the one who serves you best will be your leader. Out in the world the master sits at the table and is served by his servants! But not here! For I am your servant! Nevertheless, since you have stood true to Me in these terrible days, and since My Father has granted Me a Kingdom, I, here and now, grant you the right to eat and drink at My table in that Kingdom; and you will sit on thrones judging the twelve tribes of Israel!"

Jesus knew on the evening of Passover Day that it would be His last night on earth before returning to His Father. During supper the Devil had already suggested to Judas Iscariot, Simon's son, that

Luke 22:16; Matthew 26:26-29; Luke 22:24-30; John 13:1,2

this was the night to carry out his plan to betray Jesus. Jesus knew that the Father had given Him everything and that He had come from God and would return to God. And how He loved His disciples! So He got up from the supper table, took off His robe, wrapped a towel around His loins, poured water into a basin, and began to wash the disciples' feet and to wipe them with the towel He had around Him.

When He came to Simon Peter, Peter said to Him, "Master, You shouldn't be washing our feet like this!"

Jesus replied, "You don't understand now why I am doing it; some day you will."

"No," Peter protested, "You shall never wash my feet!"

"But if I don't, you can't be My partner," Jesus replied.

Simon Peter exclaimed, "Then wash my hands and head as well—not just my feet!"

Jesus replied, "One who has bathed all over needs only his feet washed to be entirely clean! Now you are clean—but that isn't true of everyone here." For Jesus knew who would betray Him. That is what He meant when He said, "Not all of you are clean."

After washing their feet, He put on His robe again and sat down and asked, "Do you understand what I was doing? You call Me 'Master' and 'Lord,' and you do well to say it, for it is true. And since I,

John 13:2-14

the Lord and Teacher, have washed your feet, you ought to wash each other's feet. I have given you an example to follow: Do as I have done to you. How true it is that a servant is not greater than his master! Nor is the messenger more important than the one who sends him. You know these things—now do them! That is the path of blessing.

"I am not saying these things to all of you; I know so well each one of you I chose. The Scripture declares, 'One who eats supper with Me will betray Me,' and this will soon come true. I tell you this now so that when it happens, you will believe on Me. Truly, anyone welcoming the Holy Spirit, whom I will send, is welcoming Me. And to welcome Me is to welcome the Father who sent Me."

And as they were sitting around the table eating, Jesus said, "I solemnly declare that one of you will betray Me, one of you who is here eating with Me."

A great sadness swept over them, and one by one they asked Him, "Am I the one?"

He replied, "It is one of you twelve eating with Me now. I must die, as the prophets declared long ago; but, oh, the misery ahead for the man by whom I am betrayed. Oh, that he had never been born!"

Judas, too, had asked him, "Rabbi, am I the one?" And Jesus had told him, "Yes."

The other disciples looked at each other, wondering whom He could mean. John happened to be next to Jesus at the table since he was His close

John 13:14-20; Mark 14:18-21; Matthew 26:25; John 13:22,23

friend. Simon Peter motioned to him to ask Jesus who it was who would do this terrible deed. So he leaned around and asked Him, "Lord, who is it?"

He told him, "It is the one I honor by giving the bread dipped in the sauce." And when He had dipped it, He gave it to Judas, son of Simon Iscariot. And when he had eaten it, Satan entered into him. Then Jesus told him, "Hurry—do it now." None of the others at the table knew what Jesus meant. Some thought that since Judas was their treasurer, Jesus was telling him to go and pay for the food or to give some money to the poor. Judas left at once, going out into the night.

As soon as Judas left the room, Jesus said, "My time has come; the glory of God will soon surround Me—and God shall receive great praise because of all that happens to Me. And God shall give Me His own glory, and this so very soon.

"Dear, dear children, how brief are these moments before I must go away and leave you! Then, though you search for Me, you cannot come to Me—just as I told the Jewish leaders. And so I am giving a new commandment to you now—love each other just as much as I love you. Your strong love for each other will prove to the world that you are My disciples."

Simon Peter said, "Master, where are You going?"

And Jesus replied, "You can't go with Me now; but you will follow Me later."

John 13:23-36

"But why can't I come now?" he asked, "for I am ready to die for You."

"Simon, Simon, Satan has asked to have you, to sift you like wheat, but I have pleaded in prayer for you that your faith should not completely fail. So when you have repented and turned to Me again, strengthen and build up the faith of your brothers."

Then Jesus said to all of them, "Tonight you will all desert Me. For it is written in the Scriptures that God will smite the Shepherd, and the sheep of the flock shall be scattered. But after I have been brought to life again, I will go to Galilee, and meet you there."

Peter said to Him, "I will never desert You, no matter what the others do!"

But Jesus said, "Peter, let Me tell you something. Between now and tomorrow morning when the rooster crows, you will deny Me three times, declaring that you don't even know Me."

"No!" Peter exploded. "Not even if I have to die with You! I'll never deny You!" And all the others vowed the same.

Then Jesus asked them, "When I sent you out to preach the Good News and you were without money, duffle bag, or extra clothes, how did you get along?"

"Fine," they replied.

"But now," He said, "take a duffle bag if you have one, and your money. And if you don't have a sword, you had better sell your clothes and buy

John 13:36,37; Luke 22:31,32; Matthew 26:31,32; Mark 14:29; Luke 22:34; Mark 14:31; Luke 22:35,36

one! For the time has come for this prophecy about Me to come true: 'He will be condemned as a criminal!' Yes, everything written about Me by the prophets will come true."

"Master," they replied, "we have two swords among us!"

"Two are enough!" He said.

Luke 22:36-38

Chapter 36

Toward the Moment of Truth

"Don't be upset. Trust God—and trust Me. There are many homes up there where My Father lives, and I am going to get them ready for your coming! When they are all ready, I will come back and get you and take you with Me; then you will be where I am. I would tell you plainly if this were not so. And you know how to get where I am going."

"No, we don't," Thomas said. "We don't even know where You are going—how can we know the way?"

Jesus told him, "I am the Way—yes, and the Truth and the Life. No one can get to the Father except by means of Me. If you had known who I am, then you would have known who My Father is! From now on you know Him—and have seen Him!"

Philip said, "Sir, show us the Father and we will be satisfied."

Jesus replied, "Don't you even yet know who I am, Philip, even after all this time I have been with you? Anyone who has seen Me has seen the Father! So why are you asking to see Him? Don't you believe that I am in the Father and the Father is in Me? The words I say are not My own, but are from

John 14:1-10

My Father who lives in Me! And He does His work through Me. Just believe it—that I am in the Father and the Father is in Me. Or else believe it because of the mighty miracles you have seen Me do.

"In solemn truth I tell you, anyone believing in Me shall do the same miracles I have done, and even greater ones, because I am going to be with the Father. You can ask Him for anything, using My name, and I will do it, for this will bring praise to the Father because of what I, the Son, will do for you. Yes, ask anything, using My name, and I will do it!

"If you love Me, obey Me; and I will ask the Father and He will give you another Comforter, and He will never leave you! He is the Holy Spirit, the Spirit who leads into all truth. The world at large cannot receive Him, for it isn't looking for Him and doesn't recognize Him. But you do, for He lives with you now and some day shall be in you!

"No, I will not abandon you or leave you orphans in the storm—I will come to you! In just a little while I will be gone from the world, but I will still be present with you. For I will live again—and you will too. When I come back to life again, you will know that I am in My Father, and you in Me, and I in you. The one who obeys Me is the one who loves Me; and because he loves Me, My Father will love him; and I will too, and I will reveal Myself to him."

John 14:10-22

Judas (not Judas Iscariot, but His other disciple with that name) said to Him, "Sir, why are You going to reveal Yourself only to us disciples and not to the world at large?"

Jesus replied, "Because I will only reveal Myself to those who love Me and obey Me. The Father will love them too, and We will come to them and live with them. But the world neither loves Me nor obeys Me. And remember, I am not making up this answer to your question! It is the answer given by the Father who sent Me.

"I am telling you these things now while I am still with you. But when the Father sends the Comforter to represent Me—and by the Comforter I mean the Holy Spirit—He will teach you much more as well as remind you of everything I Myself have told you.

"I am leaving you with a gift—peace of mind and heart! And the peace I give isn't fragile like the peace the world gives! So don't be troubled or afraid. Remember what I told you—I am going away, but I will come back again to you. If you really love Me, you will be very happy for Me, for now I can go to the Father, who is greater than I am. I have told you these things before they happen so that when they do, you will believe in Me.

"I don't have much more time to talk to you, for the evil prince of this world is on the way. He has no power over Me, but I will freely do what the Father requires of Me so that the world will know

John 14:22-31

that I love the Father. Come, let's be going." Then they sang a hymn and went out to the Mount of Olives.

"I am the true Vine, and My Father is the Gardener. He lops off every branch that doesn't produce. And those that bear fruit He prunes for even larger crops. He has already tended you by pruning you back for greater strength and usefulness by means of the commands I gave you.

"Take care to live in Me, and let Me live in you. For a branch can't produce fruit when severed from the vine! Nor can you be fruitful apart from Me. Yes, I am the Vine; you are the branches. Whoever lives in Me and I in him shall produce a large crop of fruit. For apart from Me you can't do a thing.

"If anyone separates from Me, he is thrown away like a useless branch, withers and is gathered into a pile with all the others and burned. But if you stay in Me and obey My commands, you may ask any request you like, and it will be granted! My true disciples produce bountiful harvests. This brings great glory to My Father.

"I have loved you even as the Father has loved Me. Live within My love. When you obey Me, you are living in My love, just as I obey My Father and live in His love. I have told you this so you will be filled with My joy. Yes, your cup of joy will overflow! I demand that you love each other as much as I love you! And here is how to measure it —the greatest love is when a person lays down his

Mark 14:26; John 15:1-14

life for his friends; and you are My friends if you obey Me. I no longer call you slaves, for a master doesn't confide in his slaves; now you are My friends, proved by the fact that I have told you everything the Father told Me.

"You didn't choose Me! I chose you! I appointed you to go and produce lovely fruit always, so that no matter what you ask for from the Father, using My name, He will give it to you. I demand that you love each other, for you get enough hate from the world! But then, it hated Me before it hated you! The world would love you if you belonged to it; but you don't—for I chose you to come out of the world, and so it hates you!

"Do you remember what I told you? 'A slave isn't greater than his master!' Since they persecuted Me, naturally they will persecute you. And if they listened to Me, they will listen to you! The people of the world will persecute you because you belong to Me, for they don't know God who sent Me. They would not be guilty unless I had come and spoken to them. But now they have no excuse for their sin.

"Anyone hating Me is also hating My Father. If I hadn't done such mighty miracles among them, they would not be counted guilty. But as it is, they saw these miracles and yet they hated both of us—Me and My Father. This has fulfilled what the prophets said concerning the Messiah, 'They hated Me without reason.' But I will send you the Comforter—the Holy Spirit, the source of all truth.

John 15:14-26

He will come to you from the Father, and will tell you all about Me. And you also must tell everyone about Me, because you have been with Me from the beginning.

"I have told you these things so that you won't be staggered by all that lies ahead. For you will be excommunicated from the synagogue, and indeed the time is coming when those who kill you will think they are doing God a service. This is because they have never known the Father or Me.

"Yes, I'm telling you these things now so that when they happen, you will remember I warned you. I didn't tell you earlier since I would still be with you for a while. But now I am going away to the one who sent Me; and none of you is interested in the purpose of My going and none of you seems to wonder why. Instead you are only filled with sorrow at My going. But the fact of the matter is that it is best for you that I go away, for if I don't, the Comforter won't come. If I do, He will—for I will send Him to you.

"And when He has come, He will convince the world of its sin, and of the availability of God's goodness, and of deliverance from judgment. Its sin is unbelief in Me; there is righteousness available because I go to the Father and you shall see Me no more; there is deliverance from judgment because the prince of this world has already been judged.

"Oh, there is so much more I want to tell you, but you can't understand it all now. When the Holy

John 15:26,27; John 16:1-13

Spirit, who is truth, comes, He shall guide you into all truth, for He will not be presenting His own ideas but passing on to you what He has heard. He will tell you about the future. He shall praise Me and bring Me great honor by showing you My glory. All the Father's glory is Mine; this is what I mean when I say that He will show you My glory. In just a little while I will be gone, and you will see Me no more; but just a little while after that, and you will see Me again!"

"Whatever is He saying?" some of His disciples asked. "What is this about 'going to the Father'? We don't know what He means!"

Jesus realized they wanted to ask Him, so He said, "Are you asking yourselves what I mean? Truly I tell you, the world will rejoice over what is going to happen to Me, and you will weep. But your weeping shall suddenly be turned to wonderful joy when you see Me again. It will be the same joy as that of a woman in labor when her child is born—her anguish gives place to rapturous joy and the pain is forgotten. You have sorrow now, but I will see you again and then you will rejoice; and no one can rob you of that joy.

"At that time you won't need to ask Me for anything, for you can go directly to the Father and ask Him, and He will give you what you ask for because you use My name. You haven't tried this before, but begin now. Ask, using My name, and you will receive and your cup of joy will overflow. I

John 16:13-25

have spoken of these matters very guardedly, but the time will come when this will not be necessary and I will tell you plainly all about the Father. Then you will present your petitions over My signature! And I won't need to ask the Father to grant you these requests, for the Father Himself loves you dearly because you love Me and believe that I came from the Father. Yes, I came from the Father into the world and will leave the world and return to the Father."

"At last You are speaking plainly," His disciples said, "and not in riddles. Now we understand that You know everything and don't need anyone to tell You anything. From this we believe that You came from God."

"Do you finally believe this?" Jesus asked. "But the time is coming—in fact, it is here—when you will be scattered, each one returning to his own home, leaving Me alone. Yet I will not be alone, for the Father is with Me. I have told you all this so that you will have peace of heart and mind. Here on earth you will have many trials and sorrows; but cheer up, for I have overcome the world."

John 16:25-33

Chapter 37

Conversation of Father and Son

When Jesus had finished saying all these things, He looked up to heaven and said, "Father, the time has come. Reveal the glory of Your Son so that He can give the glory back to You. For You have given Him authority over every man and woman in all the earth. He gives eternal life to each one You have given Him. And this is the way to have eternal life—by knowing You, the only true God, and Jesus Christ, the one You sent to earth!

"I brought You glory here on earth by doing everything You told Me to. And now, Father, reveal My glory as I stand in Your presence, the glory We shared before the world began. I have told these men all about You. They were in the world, but then You gave them to Me. Actually, they were always Yours, and You gave them to Me; and they have obeyed You. Now they know that everything I have is a gift from You, for I have passed on to them the commands You gave Me; and they took them and know of a certainty that I came down to earth from You, and they believe You sent Me.

"My plea is not for the world, but for these You have given Me, because they belong to You. And all of them, since they are Mine, belong to You; and You have given them back to Me, with every-

John 17:1-10

thing else of Yours, and so they are My glory! Now I am leaving the world, and leaving them behind, and coming to You. Holy Father, keep them in Your own care—all those You have given Me—so that they will be united just as We are, with none missing.

"During My time here I have kept safe within Your family all of these You gave to Me. I guarded them so that not one perished, except the son of hell, as the Scriptures foretold. And now I am coming to You. I have told them many things while I was with them so that they would be filled with My joy. I have given them Your commands. And the world hates them because they don't fit in with it, just as I don't. I'm not asking You to take them out of the world, but to keep them safe from Satan's power. They are not part of this world any more than I am.

"Make them pure and holy through teaching them Your words of truth. As You sent Me into the world, I am sending them into the world, and I consecrate Myself to meet their need for growth in truth and holiness. I am not praying for these alone, but also for all future believers who will come to Me because of the testimony of these. My prayer for all of them is that they will be of one heart and mind, just as You and I are, Father—that just as You are in Me and I am in You, so they will be in Us.

"I have given them the glory You gave Me—the

John 17:10-22

glorious unity of being one, as We are—I in them and You in Me, all being perfected into one—so that the world will know You sent Me and will understand that You love them as much as You love Me. Father, I want them with Me—these You've given Me—so they can see My glory. You gave Me the glory because You loved Me before the world began! O righteous Father, the world doesn't know You, but I do; and these disciples know You sent Me. And I have revealed You to them, and will keep on revealing You so that the mighty love You have for Me may be in them, and I in them."

After saying these things Jesus crossed the Kidron ravine with His disciples and entered a grove of olive trees called the Garden of Gethsemane, and He instructed His disciples, "Sit here, while I go and pray."

He took Peter, James and John with Him and began to be filled with horror and deepest distress. And He said to them, "My soul is crushed by sorrow to the point of death; stay here and watch with Me." And He went forward a little, and fell face downward on the ground, and prayed, "My Father! If it is possible, let this cup be taken away from Me. Nevertheless, I want Your will, not Mine."

Then an angel from heaven appeared and strengthened Him, for He was in such agony of spirit that He broke into a sweat of blood, with

John 17:22-26; John 18:1; Mark 14:32-34; Matthew 26:39; Luke 22:43,44 great drops falling to the ground as He prayed more and more earnestly.

At last He stood up again and returned to the three disciples and found them asleep. "Simon!" He said. "Asleep? Couldn't you watch with Me for even an hour? Watch with Me and pray, lest the Tempter overpower you. For though the spirit is willing enough, the body is weak."

Again He left them and prayed, "My Father! If this cup cannot go away until I drink it all, Your will be done."

He returned to them again and found them sleeping, for their eyes were heavy, so He went back to prayer the third time, saying the same things again.

Then He came back to the disciples and said to them, "Sleep on now and take your rest. But no! The time has come! I am betrayed into the hands of evil men! Up! Let's be going! Look! Here comes the man who is betraying Me!"

Luke 22:44,45; Mark 14:37,38; Matthew 26:42-46

Chapter 38

Betrayed! Forsaken! Denied!

Judas, the betrayer, knew the place, for Jesus had gone there many times with His disciples. The chief priests and Pharisees had given Judas a squad of soldiers and police to accompany him. Now, with blazing torches, lanterns and weapons, they arrived at the olive grove. Jesus fully realized all that was going to happen to Him. Stepping forward to meet them He asked, "Who are you looking for?"

"Jesus of Nazareth," they replied.

"I am He," Jesus said. And as He said it, they all fell backwards to the ground!

Once more He asked them, "Who are you searching for?"

And again they replied, "Jesus of Nazareth."

"I told you I am He," Jesus said; "and since I am the one you are after, let these others go." He did this to carry out the prophecy He had just made, "I have not lost a single one of those You gave Me . . ."

Judas had told the men, "You will know which one to arrest when I go over and embrace Him. Then you can take Him easily." So now Judas came straight to Jesus, "Master," he exclaimed, and embraced Him with a great show of friendliness and kissed Him on the cheek.

John 18:2-9; Mark 14:44; Matthew 26:49; Mark 14:45; Luke 22:47,48

But Jesus said, "Judas, how can you do this—betray the Messiah with a kiss?" Then the mob arrested Jesus and held Him fast.

When the other disciples saw what was about to happen, they exclaimed, "Master, shall we fight? We brought along the swords!" Then Simon Peter drew a sword and slashed off the right ear of Malchus, the High Priest's servant.

But Jesus said to Peter, "Don't resist anymore. Put away your sword. Those using swords will get killed. Shall I not drink from the cup the Father has given Me? Don't you realize that I could ask My Father for thousands of angels to protect us, and He would send them instantly? But if I did, how would the Scriptures be fulfilled that describe the events now happening?" And He touched the place where the man's ear had been and restored it.

Then Jesus spoke to the crowd: "Am I some dangerous criminal," He asked, "that you had to arm yourselves with swords and clubs before you could arrest Me? I was with you teaching daily in the Temple and you didn't stop Me then. But this is your moment—the time when Satan's power reigns supreme! This is all happening to fulfill the words of the prophets as recorded in the Scriptures." At that point, all the disciples deserted Him and fled.

There was, however, a young man following along behind, clothed only in a linen nightshirt. The mob tried to grab him, but he escaped. His

Luke 22:48; Mark 14:46; Luke 22:49; John 18:10, 11; Matthew 26:52; John 18:11; Matthew 26:53,54; Luke 22:51; Matthew 26:55; Luke 22:53; Matthew 26:56; Mark 14:51,52

clothes were torn off in the process, so that he ran away completely naked.

First they took Him to Annas, the father-in-law of Caiaphas, the High Priest that year. Caiaphas was the one who told the other Jewish leaders, "Better that one should die for all."

Friday, 3:00-6:00 A.M.

Meanwhile Peter was following far to the rear, and came to the courtyard of the High Priest's house as did another of the disciples who was acquainted with the High Priest. So that disciple was permitted into the courtyard along with Jesus, while Peter stood outside the gate. Then the other disciple spoke to the girl watching at the gate, and she let Peter in.

The girl asked Peter, "Aren't you one of Jesus' disciples?"

"No," he said, "I am not!"

The police and the household servants were standing around a fire they had made, for it was cold. And Peter stood there with them, warming himself.

Inside, the High Priest began asking Jesus about His followers and what He had been teaching them. Jesus replied, "What I teach is widely known, for I have preached regularly in the synagogue and Temple; I have been heard by all the Jewish leaders

John 18:13,14; Matthew 26:58; John 18:15-21

and teach nothing in private that I have not said in public. Why are you asking Me this question? Ask those who heard Me. You have some of them here. They know what I said."

One of the soldiers standing there struck Jesus with his fist. "Is that the way to answer the High Priest?" he demanded.

"If I lied, prove it," Jesus said. "Should you hit a man for telling the truth?"

Then Annas sent Jesus, bound, to Caiaphas the High Priest.

The chief priests and, in fact, the entire Jewish Supreme Court assembled there and looked for witnesses who would lie about Jesus, in order to build a case against Him that would result in a death sentence. But even though they found many false witnesses, these always contradicted each other, until they found two men who said, "We heard Him say, 'I will destroy this Temple made with human hands and in three days I will build another, made without human hands!'" But even they couldn't get their stories straight!

Then the High Priest stood up and said to Jesus, "Well, what about it? Did You say that, or didn't You?" But Jesus remained silent. Then the High Priest said to Him, "I demand in the name of the living God that You tell us whether You claim to be the Messiah, the Son of God."

"Yes," Jesus said, "I am. And in the future you will see Me, the Son of Man, sitting at the right

John 18:21-24; Matthew 26:59,60; Mark 14:58,59;
Matthew 26:62-64

hand of God and returning on the clouds of heaven."

Then the High Priest tore at his own clothing, shouting, "Blasphemy! What need have we for other witnesses? You have all heard Him say it! What is your verdict?"

They answered, "Give Him death." Then some of them began to spit at Him, and they blindfolded Him and began to hammer His face with their fists. "Who hit You that time, You prophet?" they jeered. And even the bailiffs were slapping His face as they led Him away.

Meanwhile as Simon Peter was standing by the fire, one of the household slaves of the High Priest —a relative of the man whose ear Peter had cut off —asked, "Didn't I see you out there in the olive grove with Jesus?" Again Peter denied it.

But after a while the men who had been standing there came over to him and said, "We know you are one of His disciples, for we can tell by your Galilean accent." Peter began to curse and swear. "I don't even know the man," he said. And immediately the cock crowed.

At that moment Jesus turned and looked at Peter. Then Peter remembered what He had said—"Before the rooster crows tomorrow morning, you will deny Me three times." And Peter walked out of the courtyard and started crying bitterly.

Matthew 26:65,66; Mark 14:65; John 18:25-27;
Matthew 26:73,74; Luke 22:61,62

Chapter 39

Tried and Convicted!

Friday Morning, 6:00-9:00 A.M.

Early the next morning at daybreak the Jewish Supreme Court assembled, including the chief priests and all the top religious authorities of the nation. Jesus was led before this council and instructed to state whether or not He claimed to be the Messiah. But He replied, "If I tell you, you won't believe Me or let Me present My case. But the time is soon coming when I, the Son of Man, shall be enthroned beside Almighty God."

They all shouted, "Then You claim You are the Son of God?"

And He replied, "Yes, I am."

"What need do we have for other witnesses?" they shouted, "for we ourselves have heard Him say it." Then the entire council took Jesus over to Pilate, the governor.

About that time Judas, who betrayed Him, when he saw that Jesus had been condemned to die, changed his mind and deeply regretted what he had done, and brought back the money to the chief priests and other Jewish leaders.

"I have sinned," he declared, "for I betrayed an innocent man."

Luke 22:66-71; Luke 23:1; Matthew 27:3,4

"That's your problem," they retorted. Then he threw the money onto the floor of the Temple and went out and hanged himself.

The chief priests picked the money up. "We can't put it in the collection," they said, "since it's against our laws to accept money paid for murder." They talked it over and finally decided to buy a certain field, where the clay was used by potters, and to make it into a cemetery for foreigners who died in Jerusalem. That is why the cemetery is still called "The Field of Blood."

This fulfilled the prophecy of Jeremiah which says, "They took the thirty pieces of silver—the price at which He was valued by the people of Israel—and purchased a field from the potters; as the Lord directed me."

Jesus' trial before Caiaphas ended in the early hours of the morning; next He was taken in chains to the palace of the Roman governor. His accusers wouldn't go in themselves for that would "defile" them, they said, and they wouldn't be allowed to eat the Passover lamb. So Pilate, the governor, went out to them and asked, "What is your charge against this man? What are you accusing Him of doing?"

They replied, "We wouldn't have brought Him to you if He weren't a criminal!"

"Then take Him away and judge Him yourselves by your own laws," Pilate told them.

"But we want Him crucified," they said, "and

Matthew 27:4-10; John 18:28; Matthew 27:2; John 18:28-31

your approval is required." This fulfilled Jesus' prediction concerning the method of His execution.

Then Pilate went back into the palace and called for Jesus to be brought to him, "Are You the King of the Jews?" he asked Him.

"'King' as you use the word or as the Jews use it?" Jesus asked.

"Am I a Jew?" Pilate retorted. "Your own people and their chief priests brought You here. Why? What have You done?"

Then Jesus answered, "I am not an earthly king. If I were, My followers would have fought when I was arrested by the Jewish leaders. But My Kingdom is not of the world."

Pilate replied, "But You are a King then?"

"Yes," Jesus said. "I was born for that purpose. And I came to bring truth to the world. All who love the truth are My followers."

"What is truth?" Pilate exclaimed. Then he went out again to the people and told them, "He is not guilty of any crime."

Then the chief priests accused Him of many crimes, and Pilate asked Him, "Why don't You say something? What about all these charges against You?" But Jesus said nothing more, much to Pilate's amazement.

The priests became desperate! "But He is causing riots against the government everywhere He goes, all over Judea, from Galilee to Jerusalem!"

"Is He then a Galilean?" Pilate asked. When they

John 18:31-38; Mark 15:3-5; Luke 23:5-7

told him yes, Pilate said to take Him to King Herod, for Galilee was under Herod's jurisdiction; and Herod happened to be in Jerusalem at the time.

Herod was delighted at the opportunity to see Jesus, for he had heard a lot about Him and had been hoping to see Him perform a miracle. He asked Jesus question after question, but there was no reply. Meanwhile the chief priests and the other religious leaders stood there shouting their accusations.

Now Herod and his soldiers began mocking and ridiculing Jesus; and putting a kingly robe on Him, they sent Him back to Pilate. That day Herod and Pilate—enemies before—became fast friends.

Then Pilate called together the chief priests and other Jewish leaders, along with the people, and announced his verdict: "You brought this man to me, accusing Him of leading a revolt against the Roman government. I have examined Him thoroughly on this point and find Him innocent. Herod came to the same conclusion and sent Him back to us—nothing this man has done calls for the death penalty."

Now the governor's custom was to release one Jewish prisoner each year during the Passover celebration, anyone they wanted. This year there was a particularly notorious criminal in jail named Barabbas. He was in prison with others for murdering a man during an insurrection. And as the crowds

Luke 23:7-15; Matthew 27:15, 16; Mark 15:7; Matthew 27:17

gathered before Pilate's house that morning he asked them, "Which shall I release to you—Barabbas, or Jesus, your Messiah?" For he knew very well that the Jewish leaders had arrested Jesus out of envy because of His popularity with the people.

Just then, as he was presiding over the court, Pilate's wife sent him this message: "Leave that good man alone; for I had a terrible nightmare concerning Him last night."

Meanwhile the chief priests and Jewish officials persuaded the crowds to ask for Barabbas' release, and for Jesus' death. So when the governor said again, "Which of these two shall I release to you?"

The crowd replied, "Barabbas!"

"Then what shall I do with Jesus, your Messiah?" Pilate asked.

And they shouted, "Crucify Him!"

"Why?" Pilate demanded. "What has He done wrong?"

But they kept shouting, "Crucify! Crucify!"

Now a mighty roar rose from the crowd as with one voice they shouted, "Kill Him, and release Barabbas to us!" Pilate argued with them, for he wanted to release Jesus. But they shouted, "Crucify Him! Crucify Him!"

Once more, for the third time, he demanded, "Why? What crime has He committed? I have found no reason to sentence Him to death. I will therefore scourge Him and let Him go."

Pilate laid open Jesus' back with a leaded whip,

Matthew 27:17-23; Luke 23:17,18, 20-22; John 19:1

and the soldiers made a crown of thorns and placed it on His head and robed Him in royal purple. Then they bowed low before Him. "Hail, 'King of the Jews!'" they mocked, and struck Him with their fists.

Pilate went outside again and said to the Jews, "I am going to bring Him out to you now, but understand clearly that I find Him not guilty."

Jesus came out wearing the crown of thorns and the purple robe. And Pilate said, "Behold the Man!" At sight of Him the chief priests and Jewish officials began yelling, "Crucify! Crucify!"

"You crucify Him," Pilate said. "I find Him not guilty."

They replied, "By our laws He ought to die because He called Himself the Son of God."

When Pilate heard this, he was more frightened than ever. He took Jesus back into the palace again and asked Him, "Where are You from?" But Jesus gave no answer.

"You won't talk to me?" asked Pilate. "Don't you realize that I have the power to release You or to crucify You?"

Then Jesus said, "You would have no power at all over Me unless it were given to you from above! So those who brought Me to you have the greater sin."

Then Pilate tried to release Him, but the Jewish leaders told him, "If you release this man, you are no friend of Caesar's. Anyone who declares himself

John 19:2-12

a king is a rebel against Caesar." At these words Pilate brought Jesus out to them again and sat down at the judgment bench on the stone-paved platform.

It was now about noon of the day before Passover. And Pilate said to the Jews, "Here is your King!"

"Away with Him," they yelled. "Away with Him—crucify Him!"

"What? Crucify your King?" Pilate asked.

"We have no king but Caesar," the chief priests shouted back.

When Pilate saw that he wasn't getting anywhere, and that a riot was developing, he sent for a bowl of water and washed his hands before the crowd, saying, "I am innocent of the blood of this good man. The responsibility is yours!"

And the mob yelled back, "His blood be on us and on our children!"

Then Pilate released Barabbas. And he gave Jesus to them to crucify Him.

John 19:12-15; Matthew 27:24-26; John 19:16

Chapter 40

Not Really the End

Friday morning, April 7, A.D. 30

The Roman soldiers took Him into the barracks of the palace, and called out the entire palace guard. They stripped Him and put a scarlet robe on Him, and made a crown from long thorns and put it on His head, and placed a stick in His right hand, and then kneeling in mockery before Him, said, "Hail, King of the Jews." And they spat on Him and grabbed the stick and beat Him on the head with it. After the mockery, they took off the robe and put His own garment on Him again, and took Him out to crucify Him.

As the crowd led Jesus away to His death, Simon of Cyrene, who was just coming into Jerusalem from the country, was forced to follow, carrying Jesus' cross.

Great crowds trailed along behind, and many grief-stricken women. But Jesus turned and said to them, "Daughters of Jerusalem, don't weep for Me, but for yourselves and for your children. For the days are coming when the women who have no children will be counted fortunate indeed. Mankind will beg the mountains to fall on them and crush them and the hills to bury them. For if such things

Mark 15:16; Matthew 27:28-31; Luke 23:26-31

as this are done to Me, the Living Tree, what will they do to you?"

And they brought Jesus to a place called Golgotha. The name means Place of a Skull. There the soldiers gave Him drugged wine to drink, but when He had tasted it, He refused. And when they had crucified Him, they threw dice to divide His clothes among them. Then they sat around and watched Him as He hung there. "Father, forgive these people," Jesus said, "for they don't know what they are doing."

It was about nine o'clock in the morning when the crucifixion took place. Two robbers were also crucified that morning. Their crosses were on either side of His. And so the Scripture was fulfilled that said, "He was counted among evil men."

And Pilate posted a sign above Him reading, "JESUS OF NAZARETH, THE KING OF THE JEWS." The place where Jesus was crucified was near the city; and the signboard was written in Hebrew, Latin and Greek, so that many people read it.

Then the chief priests said to Pilate, "Change it from 'The King of the Jews' to 'He said, I am King of the Jews.' "

Pilate replied, "What I have written, I have written. It stays exactly as it is."

When the soldiers had crucified Jesus, they put his garments into four piles, one for each of them. But they said, "Let's not tear up His robe," for it

Luke 23:31; Mark 15:22; Matthew 27:34-36; Luke 23:34; Mark 15:25,27,28; John 19:19-24 was seamless. "We'll throw dice to see who gets it." This fulfilled the Scripture that says, "They divided My clothes among them, and cast lots for My robe" (Psalm 22:18). And that is what they did.

And the people passing by hurled abuse, shaking their heads at Him and saying, "So! You can destroy the Temple and build it again in three days, can You? Well then, come on down from the cross if You are the Son of God!"

And the chief priests and Jewish leaders mocked Him too. "He saved others," they scoffed, "but He can't save Himself! So You are the King of Israel, are You? Come down from the cross and we'll believe You! He trusted God—let God show His approval by delivering Him! Didn't He say, 'I am God's Son'?"

One of the criminals hanging beside Him scoffed, "So You're the Messiah, are You? Prove it by saving Yourself—and us too, while You're at it!"

But the other criminal protested. "Don't you even fear God when you are dying? We deserve to die for our evil deeds, but this man hasn't done one thing wrong." Then he said, "Jesus, remember me when You come into Your Kingdom."

And Jesus replied, "Today you will be with Me in Paradise. This is a solemn promise."

Standing near the cross were Jesus' mother, Mary, His aunt, the wife of Cleopas, and Mary Magdalene. When Jesus saw His mother standing beside John—His close friend—He said to her, "He

John 19:24,25; Matthew 27:39-43; Luke 23:39-43;
John 19:25,26

is your son." And to John He said, "She is your mother!" And from then on he took her into his home.

About noon, darkness fell across the entire land, lasting until three o'clock that afternoon. About three o'clock, Jesus shouted, "Eli, Eli, lama sabachthani," which means, "My God, My God, why have You forsaken Me?"

Some of the bystanders misunderstood and thought He was calling for Elijah! One of them ran and filled a sponge with sour wine and put it on a stick and held it up to Him to drink. But the rest said, "Leave Him alone. Let's see whether Elijah will come and save Him!"

Jesus knew that everything was now finished, and to fulfill the Scriptures said, "I'm thirsty." A jar of sour wine was sitting there, so a sponge was soaked in it and put on a hyssop branch and held up to His lips. When Jesus had tasted it, He said, "It is finished." Then Jesus shouted out again, "Father, I commit My spirit to You," and He dismissed His spirit, and died.

And look! The curtain secluding the Holiest Place in the Temple was split apart from top to bottom; and the earth shook, and rocks broke. And tombs opened and many godly men and women who had died came back to life again, and left the cemetery after Jesus' resurrection, and went into Jerusalem, and appeared to many.

John 19:26-27; Mark 15:33; John 19:28-30; Matthew 27:50; Luke 23:46; Matthew 27:51-53

When the captain of the Roman military unit handling the executions saw what had happened and how He dismissed His spirit, he was stricken with awe before God and said, "Surely this man was innocent. This was God's Son."

And when the crowd that came to see the crucifixion saw that Jesus was dead, they went home in deep sorrow.

Some women were there, watching from a distance—Mary Magdalene; Mary (the mother of James the Younger and of Joses); Salome, the mother of James and John (the sons of Zebedee); and others. They and many other Galilean women who were His followers had ministered to Him when He was up in Galilee; and they had come with Him to Jerusalem.

The Jewish leaders didn't want the victims hanging there the next day, which was the Sabbath and a very special Sabbath at that, for it was the Passover, so they asked Pilate to order the legs of the men broken, to hasten death; then their bodies could be taken down. So the soldiers came and broke the legs of the two men crucified with Jesus; but when they came to Him, they saw that He was dead already, and they didn't break His legs. However, one of the soldiers pierced His side with a spear, and blood and water flowed out.

The soldiers did this in fulfillment of the Scripture that says, "Not one of His bones shall be

Luke 23:47; Mark 15:39; Matthew 27:54; Luke 23:48; Mark 15:40; Matthew 27:56; Mark 15:41; John 19:31-34; John 19:36

broken," and, "They shall look on Him they pierced."

Afterwards Joseph of Arimathea, a member of the Jewish Supreme Court, who had been a secret disciple of Jesus for fear of the Jewish leaders, went to Pilate and boldly asked for the body of Jesus. He was a godly man who had been expecting the Messiah's coming and had not agreed with the decision and actions of the other Jewish leaders. Pilate couldn't believe that Jesus was already dead, so he called for the Roman officer in charge and asked him. The officer confirmed the fact, and Pilate told Joseph to go ahead. So he came and took away His body.

Nicodemus, the man who had come to Jesus at night, came too, bringing a hundred pounds of embalming ointment made from myrrh and aloes. Together they wrapped Jesus' body in a long linen cloth saturated with the spices, as is the Jewish custom of burial. The place of crucifixion was near a grove of trees, where there was a new tomb, never used before. And so, because of the need for haste before the Sabbath, and because the tomb was close at hand, they laid Him there and rolled a stone in front of the entrance. Both Mary Magdalene and the other Mary were sitting nearby watching. Then they went home and prepared spices and ointments to embalm Him; but by the time they were finished it was the Sabbath, so they rested all that day as required by the Jewish law.

John 19:36-38; Luke 23:50-52; Mark 15:44,45; John 19:38-42; Mark 15:46; Matthew 27:61; Luke 23:56

Saturday

The next day—at the close of the first day of the Passover ceremonies—the chief priests and Pharisees went to Pilate and told him, "Sir, that liar once said, 'After three days I will come back to life again.' So we request an order from you, sealing the tomb until the third day, to prevent His disciples from coming and stealing His body and then telling everyone He came back to life! If that happens we'll be worse off than we were at first."

"Use your own Temple police," Pilate told them. "They can guard it safely enough!" So they did, sealing the stone and leaving guards to protect it from intrusion.

Matthew 27:62-66

Chapter 41

A Promise Kept

Sunday, April 9, A.D. 30

When the Sabbath ended, Mary Magdalene, and Salome, and Mary the mother of James went out and purchased embalming spices.

Suddenly there was a great earthquake; for an angel of the Lord came down from heaven and rolled aside the stone and sat on it! His face shone like lightning and his clothing was a brilliant white. The guards shook with fear when they saw him, and fell into a dead faint.

Very early on Sunday morning the women took the ointments to the tomb—on their way they were discussing how they could ever roll aside the huge stone from the entrance. But when they arrived they looked up and saw that the stone—a very heavy one—was already moved away and the entrance was open! Mary Magdalene ran away.

The others went in—but the Lord Jesus' body was gone! They stood there puzzled, trying to think what could have happened to it. Suddenly two men appeared before them, clothed in shining robes so bright their eyes were dazzled. The women were terrified and bowed deeply before them. Then the men asked, "Why are you looking in a tomb for

Mark 16:1; Matthew 28:2-4; Luke 24:1; Mark 16:3,4; John 20:2; Luke 24:3-5 someone who is alive? He isn't here! He has come back to life again! Don't you remember what He told you back in Galilee—that the Messiah must be betrayed into the power of evil men and be crucified and that He would rise again the third day? Look, that's where His body was lying! Now go and give this message to His disciples, including Peter! Jesus is going ahead of you to Galilee. You will see Him there, just as He told you before He died."

Then they remembered. The women ran from the tomb, badly frightened, but also filled with joy, and rushed to find the disciples to give them the angel's message.

Meanwhile Mary Magdalene found Simon Peter and John and said, "They have taken the Lord's body out of the tomb, and I don't know where they have put Him!"

They ran to the tomb to see; John outran Peter and got there first and stooped and looked in and saw the linen cloth lying there, but he didn't go in. Then Simon Peter arrived and went on inside. He also saw the cloth lying there, with the swath that had covered Jesus' head, rolled up in a bundle and lying at the side. Then John went in, too, and saw, and believed that He had risen—for until then they hadn't realized that the Scriptures said He would come to life again!

They went on home, and by that time Mary had returned to the tomb and was standing outside

Luke 24:5-7; Mark 16:6,7; Luke 24:8; Matthew 28:8; John 20:2-11 crying. And as she wept, she stooped and looked in and saw two white-robed angels sitting at the head and foot of the place where the body of Jesus had lain. The angels asked her, "Why are you crying?"

She replied, "Because they have taken away my Lord, and I don't know where they have put Him." She glanced over her shoulder and saw someone standing behind her. It was Jesus, but she didn't recognize Him!

"Why are you crying?" He asked her. "Who are you looking for?"

She thought He was the gardener. "Sir," she said, "if you have taken Him away, tell me where you have put Him, and I will go and get Him."

"Mary!" Jesus said. She turned toward Him.

"Master!" she exclaimed.

"Don't touch Me," He cautioned, "for I haven't yet ascended to the Father. But go find My brothers and tell them that I ascend to My Father and your Father, My God and your God."

It was early on Sunday morning when Jesus came back to life, and the first one who saw Him was Mary Magdalene—the woman from whom He had cast out seven demons! She found the disciples mourning and weeping, and told them that she had seen Jesus and He was alive! But they didn't believe her!

As the other women were running from the tomb, suddenly Jesus was there in front of them! "Hello there!" He said. And they fell to the ground before

John 20:11-17; Mark 16:9-11; Matthew 28:9

Him, holding His feet, and worshiping Him. Then Jesus said to them, "Don't be frightened! Go tell My brothers to leave at once for Galilee, to meet Me there."

They returned to Jerusalem and told His eleven disciples—and everyone else—what had happened. But the story sounded like a fairy tale to the men—they didn't believe it.

As the women were on the way into the city, some of the Temple police who were guarding the tomb went and told the chief priests what had happened. A meeting was called with the other Jewish leaders and it was decided to bribe the police to say that Jesus' disciples came during the night while they were asleep and stole His body!

"If the governor hears about it," the council promised, "we'll persuade him to let you alone." So the police accepted the bribe and said what they were told to. Their story spread widely among the Jews, and is still believed by them to this day.

That same day, Sunday, two of Jesus' followers were walking to the village of Emmaus, seven miles out of Jerusalem. As they walked along they were talking of Jesus' death, when suddenly Jesus Himself came along and joined them and began walking beside them! But they didn't recognize Him, for God kept them from doing so.

"You seem to be in a deep discussion about something," He said. "What are you concerned about?"

Matthew 28:9,10; Luke 24:9,11; Matthew 28:11-15; Luke 24:13-17

They stopped short, sadness written across their faces. And one of them, Cleopas, replied, "You must be the only person in all Jerusalem who hasn't heard about the terrible things that happened there last week."

"What things?" Jesus asked.

"The things that happened to Jesus, the Man from Nazareth," they said. "He was a Prophet who did incredible miracles and was a mighty Teacher, highly regarded by both God and man. But the chief priests and our religious leaders arrested Him and handed Him over to the Roman government to be condemned to death, and they crucified Him.

"But we had thought He was the glorious Messiah and that He had come to rescue Israel. And now—besides all this, which happened three days ago—some women from our group of His followers were at His tomb early this morning and came back with an amazing report that His body was missing and that they had seen some angels there who had told them Jesus is alive! Some of our men ran out to see, and sure enough, Jesus' body was gone, just as the women had said."

Then Jesus said to them, "You are such foolish, foolish people! You find it so hard to believe all that the prophets wrote in the Scriptures! Wasn't it clearly predicted by the prophets that the Messiah would have to suffer these things before entering His time of glory?"

Then Jesus quoted them passage after passage

Luke 24:17-27

from the writings of the prophets, beginning with the book of Genesis and going right on through the Old Testament, explaining what the passages meant and what they said about Himself.

By this time they were nearing Emmaus and the end of their journey. Jesus would have gone farther, but they begged Him to stay the night with them, as it was getting late. So He went home with them. When they sat down to eat, He asked God's blessing on the food and then took a small loaf of bread and broke it and was passing it over to them, when suddenly—it was as though their eyes were opened—they recognized Him! And at that moment He disappeared!

They began telling each other how their hearts had felt strangely warm as He talked with them, explaining the Scriptures during the walk down the road. Within the hour they were on their way back to Jerusalem.

Luke 24:27-33

Chapter 42

Proof upon Proof

Sunday evening

The disciples and the other followers of Jesus greeted them with these words, "The Lord has really risen! He appeared to Peter!" Then the two from Emmaus told their story of how Jesus had appeared to them as they were walking along and how they had recognized Him as He was breaking the bread. And just as they were telling about it, Jesus Himself was suddenly standing there among them, and He greeted them! But the whole group was terribly frightened, thinking they were seeing a ghost!

"Why are you frightened?" He asked. "Why do you doubt that it is really I? Look at My hands! Look at My feet! You can see that it is I, Myself! Touch Me and make sure that I am not a ghost! For ghosts don't have bodies, as you see that I do!"

As He spoke, He held out His hands for them to see the marks of the nails, and showed them the wounds in His feet. Still they stood there undecided, filled with joy and doubt. Then He asked them, "Do you have anything here to eat?" They gave Him a piece of broiled fish, and He ate it as they watched!

Luke 24:34-43

He spoke to them again and said, "As the Father has sent Me, even so I am sending you." Then He breathed on them, and told them, "Receive the Holy Spirit! If you forgive anyone's sins, they are forgiven. If you refuse to forgive them, they are unforgiven."

One of the disciples, Thomas "The Twin," was not there at the time with the others. So they kept telling him, "We have seen the Lord!"

But he replied, "I won't believe it unless I see the nail wounds in His hands—and put my fingers into them—and place my hand into His side!"

Sunday, April 16, A.D. 30

Eight days later the disciples were together again, and this time Thomas was with them. The doors were locked; but suddenly, as before, Jesus was standing among them and greeting them! Then He said to Thomas, "Put your finger into My hands! Put your hand into My side! Don't be faithless any longer! Believe!"

"My Lord and my God!" Thomas said.

Then Jesus told him, "You believe because you have seen Me. But blessed are those who haven't seen Me and believe anyway!"

April, May, A.D. 30

Later Jesus appeared again to the disciples be-

John 20:21-29; John 21:1

side the Lake of Galilee. This is how it happened: A group of them were there—Simon Peter, Thomas "The Twin," Nathanael from Cana in Galilee, James and John and two other disciples.

Simon Peter said, "I'm going fishing."

"We'll come too," they all said. They did, but caught nothing all night. At dawn they saw a man standing on the beach but couldn't see who it was. He called, "Any fish, boys?"

"No," they replied.

Then He said, "Throw out your net on the right-hand side of the boat, and you'll get plenty of them!" So they did, and couldn't draw in the net because of the weight of the fish there were so many!

Then John said to Peter, "It is the Lord!" At that, Simon Peter put on his tunic, for he was stripped to the waist, and jumped into the water and swam ashore. The others stayed in the boat and dragged the loaded net to shore, about 300 feet away. When they got there, they saw that a fire was kindled and fish were frying over it, and there was bread.

"Bring some of the fish you've just caught," Jesus said. So Simon Peter went out and pulled the net ashore. He counted 153 large fish; and yet the net hadn't torn!

"Now come and have some breakfast!" Jesus said; and none of them dared ask Him if He really was the Lord, for they were quite sure of it. Then Jesus went around serving them the bread and fish.

John 21:1-13

This was the third time Jesus had appeared to them since His return from the dead.

After breakfast Jesus said to Simon Peter, "Simon, son of John, do you love Me more than these others?"

"Yes," Peter replied, "You know I am Your friend."

"Then feed My lambs," Jesus told him.

Jesus repeated the question: "Simon, son of John, do you really love Me?"

"Yes, Lord," Peter said, "You know I am Your friend!"

"Then take care of My sheep," Jesus said.

Once more He asked him, "Simon, son of John, are you really My friend?"

Peter was grieved at the way Jesus asked the question this third time. "Lord, You know my heart, You know I am," he said.

Jesus said, "Then feed My little sheep. When you were young, you were able to do as you liked and go wherever you wanted to; but when you are old, you will stretch out your hands and others will direct you and take you where you don't want to go." Jesus said this to let him know what kind of death he would die to glorify God. Then Jesus told him, "Follow Me."

Peter turned around and saw the disciple Jesus loved following, the one who had leaned around at supper that time to ask Jesus, "Master, which of us

John 21:14-20

will betray You?" Peter asked Jesus, "What about him, Lord? What sort of death will he die?"

Jesus replied, "If I want him to live until I return, what is that to you? You follow Me."

So the rumor spread among the brotherhood that that disciple wouldn't die! But that isn't what Jesus said! He only said, "If I want him to live until I come, what is that to you?"

Then the eleven disciples went to the mountain where Jesus had told them to meet Him. There they met Him and worshiped Him—but some of them weren't sure it really was Jesus!

Jesus told the disciples, "All authority in heaven and earth has been given to Me. Therefore go and make disciples in all the nations, baptizing them into the name of the Father and of the Son and of the Holy Spirit, and teaching them to obey all the commands I have given you; and be sure of this—that I am with you always, even to the end of the world."

Then He said, "When I was with you before, do you not remember My telling you that everything written about Me by Moses and the prophets and in the Psalms must all come true?" Then He opened their minds to understand at last these many Scriptures! And He said, "Yes, it was written long ago that the Messiah must suffer and die and rise again from the dead on the third day; and that this message of salvation should be taken to all nations,

John 21:20-23; Matthew 28:16-20; Luke 24:44-47

starting from Jerusalem: There is forgiveness of sins for all who turn to Me.

"You have seen these prophecies come true, and now I will send the Holy Spirit upon you, just as My Father promised."

During the 40 days after His crucifixion He appeared to the apostles from time to time in human form and proved to them in many ways that it was actually He Himself they were seeing. And on these occasions He talked to them about the Kingdom of God. In one of these meetings He told them not to leave Jerusalem until the Holy Spirit came upon them in fulfillment of the Father's promise. Jesus had spoken about this before—"John baptized you with water," He had said, "but you shall be baptized with the Holy Spirit in just a few days."

Another time when He appeared to them, they asked Him, "Lord, are You now going to free Israel from Rome and restore us as an independent nation?"

"The Father sets those dates," He replied. "They are not for you to know. But when the Holy Spirit has come upon you, you will receive power to preach with great effect about My death and resurrection to the people in Jerusalem, throughout Judea, in Samaria and to the ends of the earth."

It was not long afterwards that Jesus led them out along the road to Bethany, and lifting His hands to heaven, He blessed them. And then He rose into the sky and disappeared into a cloud,

Luke 24:47-49; Acts 1:3-9; Luke 24:50,51; Acts 1:9

leaving them staring after Him. As they were straining their eyes for another glimpse, suddenly two white-robed men were standing there among them, and they said, "Men of Galilee, why are you standing here staring at the sky? Jesus has gone away to heaven, and some day, just as He went, He will return!"

They were at the Mount of Olives at the time, so now they walked the half mile back to Jerusalem and they worshiped Him, and returned to Jerusalem, filled with mighty joy, and were continually in the Temple, praising God. And the disciples went everywhere preaching, and the Lord was with them and confirmed what they said by the miracles that followed their messages.

Acts 1:9-12; Luke 24:52,53; Mark 16:20

Conclusion

Jesus' disciples saw Him do many other miracles besides the ones told about in this book, but these are recorded so that you will believe that He is the Messiah, the Son of God, and that believing in Him you will have Life. And I suppose that if all the other events in Jesus' life were written, the whole world could hardly contain the books!

John 20:30,31; John 21:25

Appendix: Genealogies

Two of the Gospel accounts include genealogies of Jesus of Nazareth. The first traces His line through Joseph, the husband of Mary. The second is the line of Mary, the mother of Jesus. You will note that Jesus was known as the son of Joseph, Mary's husband.

Matthew 1:1-16

These are the ancestors of Jesus Christ, a descendant of King David and of Abraham. Abraham was the father of Isaac; Isaac was the father of Jacob; Jacob was the father of Judah and his brothers. Judah was the father of Perez and Zerah (Tamar was their mother); Perez was the father of Hezron; Hezron was the father of Aram; Aram was the father of Aminadab; Aminadab was the father of Nahshon; Nahshon was the father of Salmon; Salmon was the father of Boaz (Rahab was his mother); Boaz was the father of Obed (Ruth was his mother); Obed was the father of Jesse; Jesse was the father of King David. David was the father of Solomon (the ex-wife of Uriah was his mother).

Solomon was the father of Rehoboam; Rehoboam was the father of Abijah; Abijah was the father of Asa; Asa was the father of Jehosophat;

Jehosophat was the father of Joram; Joram was the father of Uzziah; Uzziah was the father of Jotham; Jotham was the father of Ahaz; Ahaz was the father of Hezekiah; Hezekiah was the father of Manasseh; Manasseh was the father of Amon; Amon was the father of Josiah; Josiah was the father of Jechoniah and his brothers (born at the time of the exile to Babylon).

After the exile: Jechoniah was the father of Shealtiel; Shealtiel was the father of Zerubbabel; Zerubbabel was the father of Abiud; Abiud was the father of Eliakim; Eliakim was the father of Azor; Azor was the father of Zadoc; Zadoc was the father of Achim; Achim was the father of Eliud; Eliud was the father of Eleazar; Eleazar was the father of Mathan; Mathan was the father of Jacob; Jacob was the father of Joseph (the husband of Mary, who was the mother of Jesus Christ, the Messiah).

Luke 3:23-38

Joseph's father was Heli; Heli's father was Matthat; Matthat's father was Levi; Levi's father was Melchi; Melchi's father was Jannai; Jannai's father was Joseph; Joseph's father was Mattathias; Mattathias' father was Amos; Amos' father was Nahum; Nahum's father was Esli; Esli's father was Naggai; Naggai's father was Maath; Maath's father was Mattathias; Mattathias' father was Semein; Semein's father was Josech; Josech's father was Joda; Joda's father was Joanan; Joanan's father was Rhesa; Rhesa's father was Zerubbabel.

Zerubbabel's father was Shealtiel; Shealtiel's father was Neri; Neri's father was Melchi; Melchi's father was Addi; Addi's father was Cosam; Cosam's father was Elmadam; Elmadam's father was Er; Er's father was Jesus; Jesus' father was Eliezer; Eliezer's father was Jorim; Jorim's father was Matthat; Matthat's father was Levi; Levi's father was Symeon; Symeon's father was Judas; Judas' father was Joseph; Joseph's father was Jonam; Jonam's father was Eliakim; Eliakim's father was Melea; Melea's father was Menna; Menna's father was Mattatha; Mattatha's father was Nathan; Nathan's father was David.

David's father was Jesse; Jesse's father was Obed; Obed's father was Boaz; Boaz's father was Salmon; Salmon's father was Nahshon; Nahshon's father was Aminadab; Aminadab's father was Admin; Admin's father was Arni; Arni's father was Hezron; Hezron's father was Perez; Perez' father was Judah; Judah's father was Jacob; Jacob's father was Isaac; Isaac's father was Abraham.

Abraham's father was Terah; Terah's father was Nahor; Nahor's father was Serug; Serug's father was Reu; Reu's father was Peleg; Peleg's father was Eber; Eber's father was Shelah; Shelah's father was Cainan; Cainan's father was Arphaxad; Arphaxad's father was Shem; Shem's father was Noah; Noah's father was Lamech; Lamech's father was Methuselah; Methuselah's father was Enoch; Enoch's father was Jared; Jared's father was Mahalaleal; Mahalaleal's father was Cainan; Cainan's father was Enos; Enos' father was Seth; Seth's father was Adam; Adam's father was God.

INDEX